ALSO FROM n+1 BOOKS:

P.S. 1 Symposium: A Practical Avant-Garde

What We Should Have Known: Two Discussions

What Was the Hipster? A Sociological Investigation

The Trouble Is the Banks: Letters to Wall Street

No Regrets: Three Discussions

Buzz: A Play

Other Russias

Canon/Archive: Studies in Quantitative Formalism

The Earth Dies Streaming: Film Writing, 2002–2018

Missing Time: Essays

The Intellectual Situation: The Best of n+1's Second Decade

THE LAST SOVIET ARTIST

Victoria Lomasko

TRANSLATED FROM THE RUSSIAN
BY BELA SHAYEVICH

n+1 BOOKS

n+1 FOUNDATION   NEW YORK

I dedicate this book to my friend the artist, poet, and curator Nadia Plungian. Her support throughout the many years I worked on the book was immensely helpful.

Text and images © 2025 Victoria Lomasko, except "Collective Shame":
text © 2022 Victoria Lomasko and art © 2022 Joe Sacco
Translation © 2025 Bela Shayevich, except "Five Steps":
translation © 2025 Mark Krotov
All rights reserved

Published 2025 by n+1 Foundation
37 Greenpoint Avenue #316, Mailbox 18
Brooklyn, New York 11222
www.nplusonemag.com

ISBN 978-1-953813-14-5

Printed by the Sheridan Press
Manufactured in the United States of America

Design by Bo-Won Keum

First Printing

"Collective Shame" *was originally published in* The New Yorker *and "Moscow Under Snow" was originally published in* The Nib. *The illustrations on pages 97 and 163 were produced by students in Victoria Lomasko's master classes.*

The Last Soviet Artist *was published with support from Furthermore: a program of the J. M. Kaplan Fund, and the Ideas Workshop of the Open Society Foundations. The n+1 Foundation's programs are made possible in part by the New York State Council on the Arts with the support of the Office of the Governor and the New York State Legislature, as well as by public funds from the New York City Department of Cultural Affairs, in partnership with the City Council.*

CONTENTS

9 Introduction

TRACES OF EMPIRE

17 A Trip to Bishkek, 2014
35 A Trip to Yerevan, 2015
61 A Trip to Dagestan, 2015
87 Travels to Tbilisi, 2015–16
135 A Trip to Ingushetia, 2017
159 Travels to Osh, 2016–17

THE LAST SOVIET ARTIST BECOMES SOMEONE ELSE

185 A Trip to Minsk, 2020
221 Moscow: A Battle of the Generations, 2021
241 Moscow: Life on the Island, 2021

EXILE

289 Moscow Under Snow
293 Collective Shame *(with Joe Sacco)*
299 Five Steps

INTRODUCTION

The Last Soviet Artist was originally conceived as a continuation of my previous book, *Other Russias*, following its path, but expanding its range into the so-called post-Soviet space.

I was running from Moscow, where, due to growing censorship and repression, it was becoming ever more dangerous and difficult to produce work about social issues. As someone who had lived in the USSR, I was also interested in seeking out the final traces of the Soviet empire and examining them closely in order to understand what it was that had once united our nations, what remained of our connections, and whether there was some kind of shared post-post-Soviet future that lay ahead of us.

The Soviet children's books and magazines I grew up on often had stories about the wonderful and indestructible friendship among the fifteen Soviet republics. These stories were accompanied by pretty pictures of the Caucasus Mountains, Asian steppes, people in colorful robes holding fruit and, of course, over and over again, fifteen children of different nationalities holding hands, dancing together in a circle.

I never visited any of the Soviet republics when I was young. In 2014, when I started traveling through the post-Soviet space, I was, to a certain degree, still under the spell of those fairytale pictures and stories from children's magazines. Every time I would come across something that reminded me of them, I'd write it down and draw it.

Otherwise, I worked the same way I had in Russia. I produced my drawings right where the events depicted in them occurred and interviewed people using methods drawn from journalism and sociology. I studied how societies seemed to be structured and how these structures affected people's lives and what kind of impact they had on various local and popular initiatives, transformations in gender roles, changes in how people interacted with public space, and so on.

At first I was determined to visit every former Soviet republic in order to make this book, but the pandemic got in the way of those plans, forcing me to reassess everything, including my artistic methods. The first part of this book collects the reportage that I completed before Covid.

In 2020, at the peak of the pandemic, a peaceful revolution began in Belarus. I decided that this was the story that was missing from my book. In all my other reporting, I had described normal, everyday life, but now here was my chance to capture the rupture of the post-Soviet space, the transformation of a post-Soviet society into something new. You could say that the alliance between Russia and Belarus is the last remaining vestige of Soviet empire and thus, had the revolution in Belarus been successful, it would have transformed the political landscape, rendering the very term "post-Soviet" obsolete.

I write about the main events I witnessed in Minsk in the seventh chapter of this book, but there was a story that didn't make it in. Before returning to Moscow, worried about my drawings, I decided to try to scan the originals, but this turned out to be a difficult task. All the copy shops fell through, and I couldn't manage to track down anyone who owned a scanner. Finally, a woman who worked at one of the state museums offered to clandestinely scan the drawings at her office. As I walked down the museum's dusty, gray corridors, so reminiscent of all the interiors from my childhood—and as I found myself jumping and frantically closing the scanning program anytime a museum employee approached (would they report me if they discovered what I was doing?)—my body remembered what it had really meant to be a Soviet person. Any remaining nostalgia I'd had for that period vanished forever at that moment.

That winter, Alexei Navalny's return to Russia and the ensuing round of mass demonstrations ended in mass repression. Between the harsh censorship of any artistic accounts of processes that were happening in front of our eyes and the inability to leave and go work in the West due to the pandemic, I was thrown back into the semblance of a Soviet reality, when the only place a nonconformist artist could escape to was her inner world.

I realized that all I had were my perceptions—that what was happening around me didn't matter. All that mattered was how sensitively I could register it. Leaving journalism and sociology behind, I discovered that I could discuss anything I wanted to using symbols and metaphors. Humming in the background of the hundreds of documentary sketches I made for the book, I discovered enormous symbols: Soviet monuments that had come to life and decided to take their revenge, young people framed by the flames of history. What became clear to me was that this book's overarching theme was generational conflict.

I finished writing and illustrating *The Last Soviet Artist* three weeks before the war began. My final days in Moscow and my first few months in Europe are the subject of the third part of the book, "Exile."

Having found myself in Europe as an émigré, I understood one very simple thing: throughout my entire life I'd worked under a dichotomy between Russia and the West. Socialism and totalitarianism, or democracy and capitalism? I suspect that that kind of insight occurs to any non-Western dissident artist who ends up as an immigrant or an exile in Europe or the United States. We're good and useful as long as we're stuck in our problematic countries, criticizing them while fostering an overarching faith in the West as the ideal model of human flourishing. While working in the post-Soviet space, I tried my best to operate as a critic of our internal reality whose angle of approach wasn't limited to European liberal positions. I tried to show that reality's multidimensionality. In immigration, that multidimensionality has no place. At first I thought that the rejection I've faced at a huge number of European institutions was the result of an effort to "cancel" Russian culture, but I now understand that the cause is deeper. Those who have fled their countries aren't meant to depict those places with complexity, in multiple colors—what is required is a simplistic black-and-white image, what one might call a European version of propaganda.

Only a few of the drawings in this book were shown at exhibitions in Europe—no one wants them. This book has thus become my own independent medium, and my publishers have proven themselves to be far more adventurous than curators at museums and galleries. *The Last Soviet Artist* has already appeared in Spanish, Catalan, French, and German; it has been translated into Mandarin, Dutch, and Hungarian; it was awarded the PEN Català Free Voice Prize and the Prix Couilles au cul pour le courage artistique, Festival international de la bande dessinée d'Angoulême. My books are now my only form of connection with a wide audience.

I'm certain that the main task of 21st-century art is to rise above the dichotomies, to model a way of inhabiting the world—a society—that will allow people with all kinds of backgrounds, from all kinds of places, to unite. This will be the subject of my next book.

ЛOMACKO

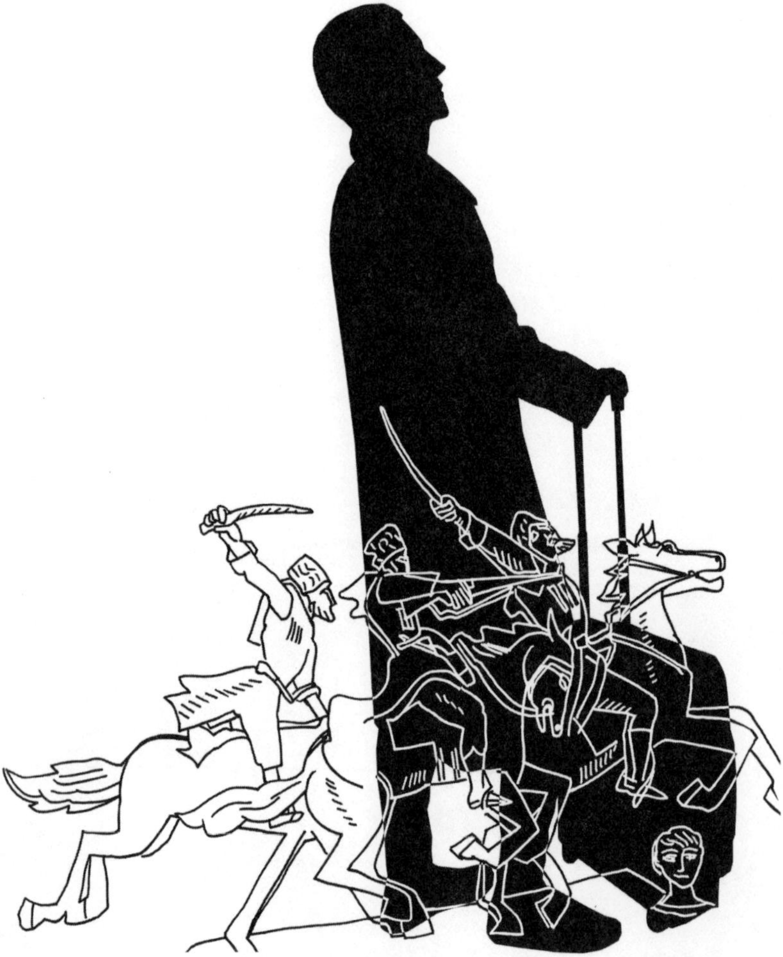

TRACES OF EMPIRE

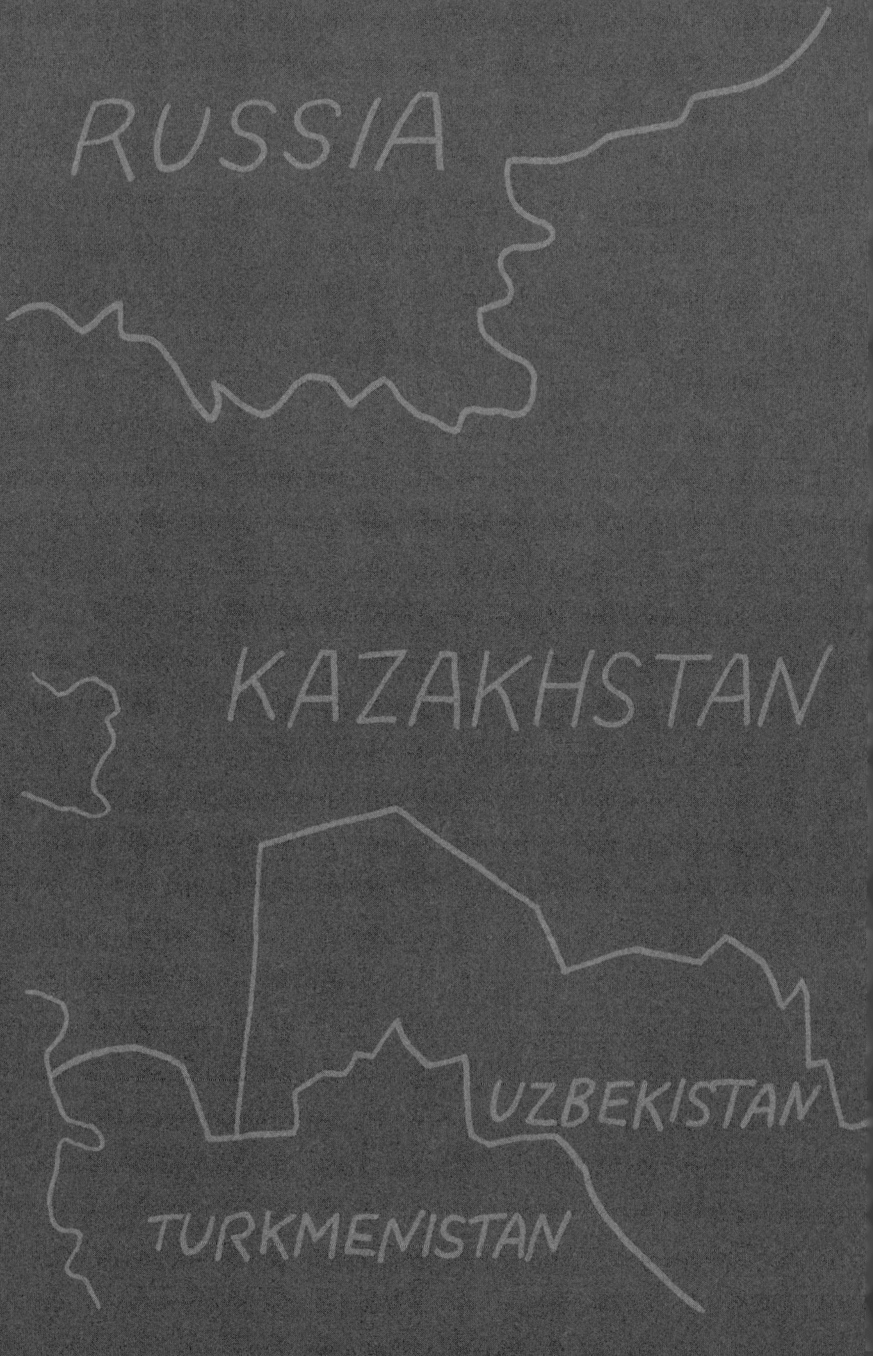
RUSSIA
KAZAKHSTAN
UZBEKISTAN
TURKMENISTAN

A TRIP TO BISHKEK, 2014

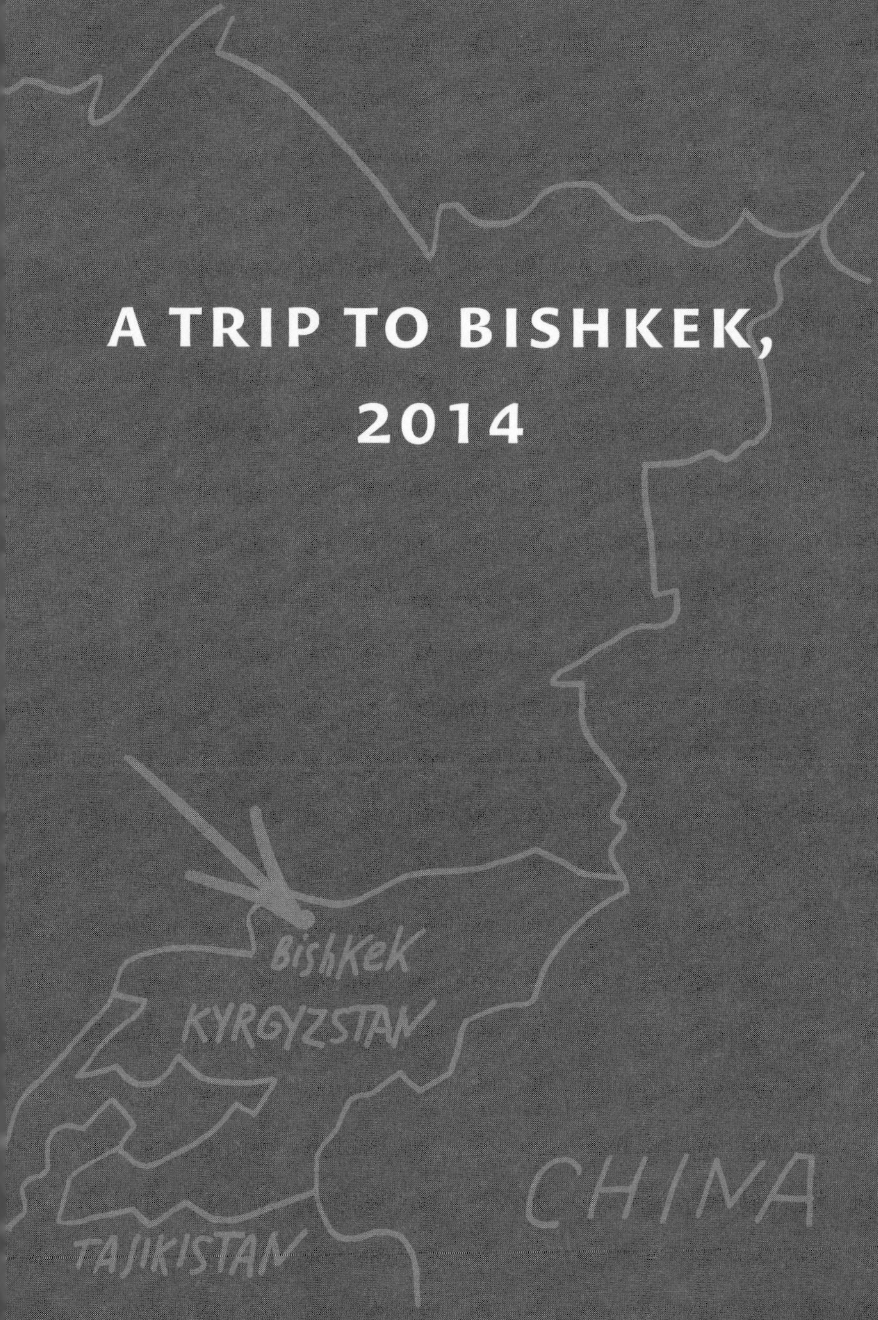
Bishkek
KYRGYZSTAN
TAJIKISTAN
CHINA

KYRGYZSTAN/KYRGYZIA

I began studying the post-Soviet space in 2014 with a trip to Bishkek. I'd been invited by a local feminist group. "Do they really have feminists in Kyrgyzia?" Moscow activists asked in surprise before my departure.

Selbi, the leader of the feminist group, corrected me several times on the way from the airport. "Don't say 'Kyrgyzia,'" she said. "It's called Kyrgyzstan. And it's not 'Kirghiz,' it's 'Kyrgyz.'" Local Russians still call it what they are used to calling it—people just ignore their i's. But when a Kyrgyz person calls themselves or others Kirghiz, it means that they've gone totally Russian and forgotten their people's traditions.

FEMINISM, KYRGYZ-STYLE

Baktygul, Daria, and Meyerim are members of Activist Girls of Kyrgyzstan. They're 13 and 14 years old. They're preparing to apply for a grant from the Frida Foundation. If they're selected, they'll use the money to hold manaschy competitions for girls.

Manaschy are orators who perform the Manas, a Kyrgyz epic poem. In the past, only men were allowed to take on this honorary role, but in recent years more girls have emerged as orators. Baktygul is one of them. She said that boys were specially trained and that their teachers sit on juries, while girls have to study on their own and have practically no chances of winning the competitions.

I asked the girls about the practice of bride kidnapping, ala kachuu. Two of them told me their mothers were kidnapped: "It was a crush from her school days. My mom wanted to keep studying, but she was forced to get married."

"My cousins kidnapped their brides," Daria told me. "This was in the 21st century. Four guys stole my cousin. She's really big, though—she tried to fight them off. They barely managed."

"Are you afraid of being kidnapped?" I asked the girls.

"No. There's a law now. We'll just say, 'What about Article 154 and 155? You want to do ten years in prison?'"

The penalties became more strict in 2013. Before that, people who kidnapped underage "brides" only faced between three and five years in prison, and if a girl was over 17 there would only be a fine. The change was brought about in part through the efforts of the Center for Women's Aid and the Open Hotline, as well as the activism of women's groups around the country. One of the most effective demonstrations was organized in the center of Bishkek by a feminist group from the capital. They put up 19,300 small flags—9,800 red ones, for all the women who had been kidnapped within a single year; 2,000 white ones, for the number of women raped during their kidnapping; and 7,500 purple ones, for the number of kidnapped women who reported experiencing domestic violence.

This is Farida, a Dungan and a member of the feminist group in Bishkek. I came to her house for Eid. At a certain point, girls are no longer brought along to other people's houses, because that's when they begin to serve, cook, and clean for the many guests that come to their homes for the celebration.

Dungan families are very big. Generations live together, and there is a strict hierarchy between the family members. Women and girls are subjugated by their domestic duties. Since she was little, Farida got used to getting up at 6 in the morning to start doing housework. She wasn't allowed out to play with other kids. "Our house was the only space where I was allowed to exist." She had to fight for her right to attend school. As Farida started to meet feminists and became involved in activism, her family began putting so much pressure on her that she was forced to run away from home. Farida was one of the main organizers of the action with the flags.

After a year of living in the feminist community, Farida returned home. Thanks to her daughter's influence, her mother Sophia also became interested in women's rights and was able to change the way their household was run.

Her younger sister Maria now has free time. She can play with other children, draw, and study.

Comments from the Kyrgyz women about this drawing:

"That's way too long!"

"My grandma gave birth in the field and went back to work right away!"

"Kyrgyz women are much braver!"

Women and children continue to work hard in Kyrgyz villages. "As soon as a child turns 6," Meyerim said, "she has to think about providing for herself. From the age of 9, she has to start paying for her textbooks and her school uniform. Teenagers are hired to pick raspberries and other berries. They work until 10 PM every night."

THE PROBLEMS OF MIGRATION

When its organizers learned that there was a famous Moscow artist in Bishkek, I was invited to draw at the Mekendeshter ("Our Countrymen") Forum, which had been organized at the behest of Roza Otunbayeva, the former president of Kyrgyzstan.

—How are we supposed to develop our country when half of our people don't live here?

The forum was dedicated to the issue of migration. The discussions took place in the roomy, beautifully designed Kyrgyz-Turkish Manas University, which was established by Turks in 1997. To the left of the stage, there was a big portrait of Ataturk, and to the right, a painting of Manas, the protagonist of the Kyrgyz saga. The program included a separate discussion of the cooperation between the "brotherly nations" of Kyrgyzstan and Turkey. In recent years, many Kyrgyz people have chosen to travel to Turkey to work because, compared to Russia, migrants are treated with greater respect there. Kyrgyzstan is growing more Islamized due to Turkish influence.

Nearly half of the forum participants presented in Russian. None of the panels were dedicated to collaboration with Russia, but the subject kept coming up. Above all, people wanted to talk about Kyrgyzstan's entry into the Eurasian Customs Union.

Entering this alliance will streamline migration into Russia and increase immigration. But forum participants pointed out that there was already a dearth of specialists living in Kyrgyzstan. In some regions, there weren't enough workers of any kind.

You can look up what Russians think about Kyrgyzstan joining the EACU. Usually they're mad about all the mooching churki, or excited about the "reunification of Russian lands." Occasionally you see liberal-minded comments like, "somebody has to do our dirty work for us," but not often.

Very often, the money earned by migrants over several years can be spent, in the matter of a month, on a toi. A *toi* is a lavish feast. The main difference between a toi and a regular celebration is that a toi has to have so much food that the guests can't finish it all and have to take some home with them. When an infant is circumcised, the family welcomes guests for an entire month. For a wedding toi, families take out lines of credit that they might spend years paying off.

The forum's closing reception took place in a suburb of Bishkek, at the impressive Supara Ethno-Complex. There was no lack of food or alcohol. The party ended around midnight, and the guests took home their leftovers in special containers.

LGBT

I like finding my way into underground spaces and being the first artist to document what happens in them. In Bishkek I visited a secret LGBT club, likely the only one in the country.

Officially, there are no LGBT people in Kyrgyzstan. Homosexuality is permitted among Russians, but not Kyrgyz people. Everyone at the club, however, was Kyrgyz. There were almost no femme couples—the lesbians in Kyrgyzstan are even more underground than the gay men.

Just as in Russia, gays, lesbians, and transgender people in Kyrgyzstan are often attacked, beaten, and raped. After the gay propaganda law passed in Russia, LGBT activists here started being attacked more often.

I talked to some of the people at the club, but I will not write about them. Bishkek is a small enough town, and any detail could prove dangerous to these individuals.

"We're constantly insulted and degraded. We can't imagine how it's going to go on in the future. How do you find someone to date? How do you come out to your parents? Or how do you keep your parents from finding out? How do you leave this club safely, without getting caught?" These are the things people said to me as I drew them.

In public discussions of the law legislating criminal liability for so-called LGBT propaganda, Kyrgyz politicians said, "We stand with Russia in defending the Eastern world from the West." It's likely that many regular citizens agree with this stance. They don't pay attention to the developments in Russia and don't realize that by letting their government impinge on the rights of one social group, they make themselves helpless to stand in the way of a whole deluge of future laws censoring and infringing on huge swaths of their private lives. It will be sad if the burgeoning civic society in Kyrgyzstan ends up facing a future like ours.

UKRAINE
Sea of Azov
RUSSIA
Black Sea
GEORGIA
ARMENIA
TURKEY

A TRIP TO YEREVAN, 2015

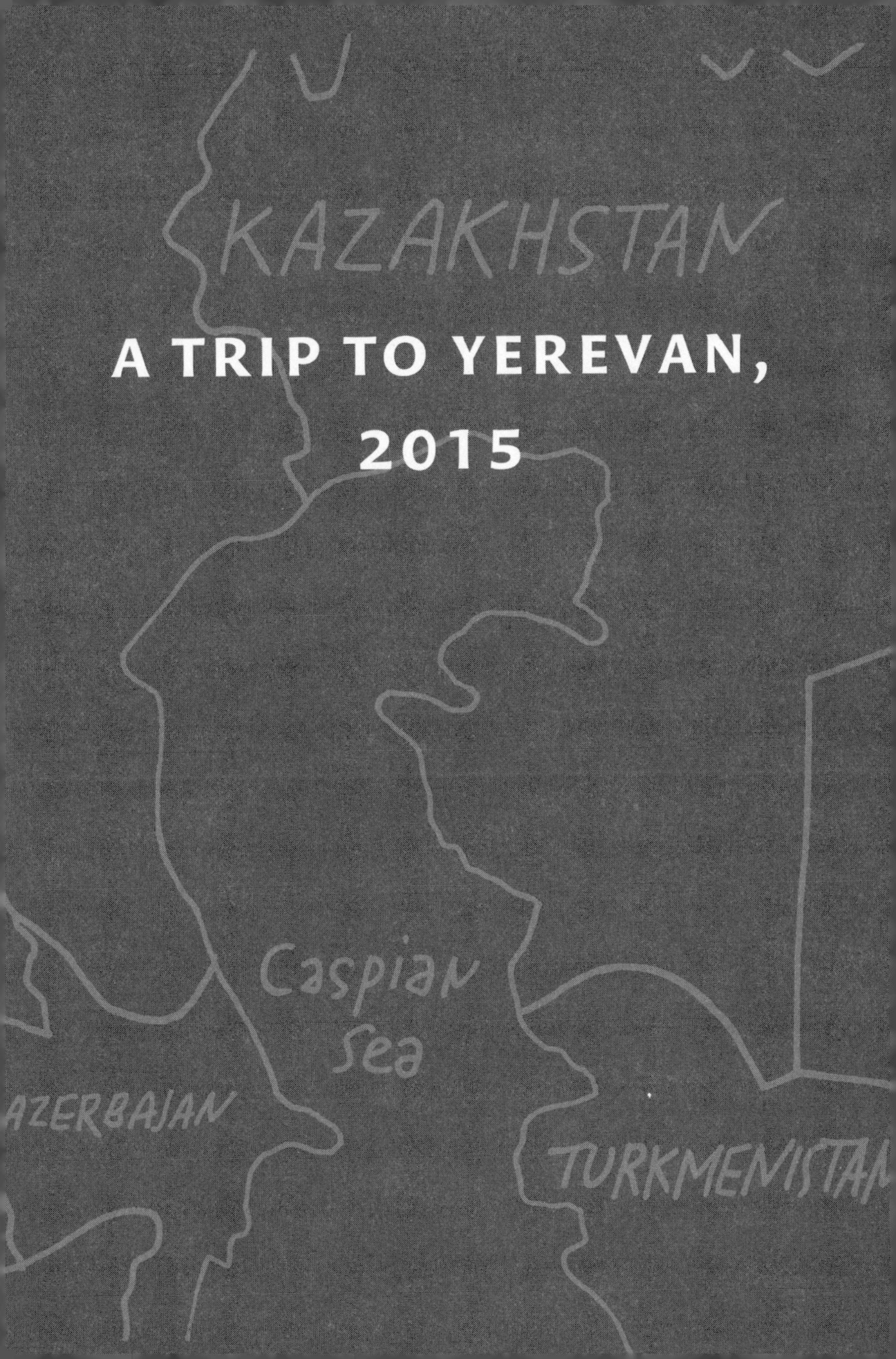
KAZAKHSTAN
Caspian Sea
AZERBAJAN
TURKMENISTAN

WHO LIVES IN YEREVAN?

I visited Armenia for the first time in 2015. The strongest impression from my first day in Yerevan was the sense that only one language was being spoken out on the street. Armenia is a monoethnic country: over 97 percent of the people are Armenians. You can pick out tourists immediately. There is no hostility toward outsiders, but the locals keep their distance. I realized that if I wanted to see the inner life of the city, I would only be able to do so with the help of Armenian friends.

This kind of urban homogeneity was so unfamiliar that I immediately started to wonder who else lives in Yerevan besides Armenians. I learned that there are small communities of Kurds, Ezids, Assyrians, Greeks, and Molokans in Yerevan that are generally closed off to outsiders. None of the Armenians I knew had any social or professional connections with anyone from these minority groups.

FRAMRZE
ارمنستان - فرامرز

The crowd on the street started seeming more diverse once I learned to distinguish Iranians from the local tourists. Armenians semi-condescendingly refer to them as Persians and claim that they come to Armenia to let off steam, get drunk, and pick up prostitutes. Every evening, a crowd of so-called Persians gathered on Republic Square to watch the singing fountains. The majority of them were easy to talk to, and so, during my first few days in Yerevan, I made a dozen portraits of Iranian men and women.

TURKS WILL ALWAYS BE TURKS

Unlike Russia, where people are alienated from one another, mutual aid and social control are cultivated in Armenian society. The notion that the Armenian nation is one big happy family is promoted by the government, which makes internal criticism of its policies more challenging. Participants in the ElectroYerevan protests against price hikes on electricity told me that the police tried to talk them down by saying, "We are all brothers and sisters here!"

The topic of the Armenian genocide comes up constantly. The very first poster I saw at the airport compared Turks to Hitler. Every evening on Northern Prospect, street musicians sing genocide-era songs about resisting the Turks. The musicians instantly find themselves surrounded by Armenians in town for the summer, who sing along passionately. During ElectroYerevan, some protesters used these as protest songs.

There's a saying in Armenia: "Turks will always be Turks"—that is, dangerous enemies. But Yerevan's progressive young people follow civic life and developments in Turkey with keen interest and sympathize with the leftist movement there. I went to an activist event where people were discussing how to quickly translate and publicize news of the anti-government actions in Turkey set off by the terrorist attack in Suruç. Official media outlets barely cover Armenia's neighbors: Turkey, Iran, Azerbaijan, and Georgia.

PUBLIC SPACE IN THE CITY

If you walk around downtown Yerevan without wandering into the inner courtyards, the city's aspirations toward sleek self-presentation might remind you of Moscow.

For the first few days, I couldn't understand where to buy cheap local produce: there weren't any fruit stalls on the street, at the grocery stores the prices weren't much different than they were in Moscow, and I had to take public transportation to get to the closest market. Only later was it explained to me that I had to seek out the privately operated sheds and kiosks in courtyards.

If you want to eat cheap, delicious food, you look for hole-in-the-wall cafes run by Syrian refugees—the restaurants run by local Armenians are more expensive. There aren't many good thrift stores in Yerevan, but there are a lot of expensive brand-name ones, just like in Moscow. In the evening, fashionable people promenade along Yerevan's biggest streets like they're walking down a runway: men with very short haircuts in dark clothes and women with long hair and elaborate makeup in tight, brightly colored outfits that show off their chests.

You can pick out the sex workers among the crowd. I watched as a fight broke out on Republic Square—a man said something demeaning to a sex worker about her profession, and she responded with something to the effect of "my body my choice."

As I was trying to draw the scene, another sex worker suddenly grabbed me and started yelling, attracting a group of pimps. Thankfully, the woman I'd been drawing saved my sketchbook and even agreed to pose for a portrait.

Sex Worker from Republic Square

You can discover a lot of interesting things in Yerevan's inner courtyards. There are, for instance, tiny private hair salons where people get haircuts, play backgammon, and talk politics. One day, as we were walking through Yerevan, we came upon one of these places, and my Armenian friends asked permission for me to draw there.

One of the regulars at the barber shop turned out to be the son of the famous socialist realist artist Simon Galstyan. He started criticizing the way that Russian language and culture had been forced on Armenians in the Soviet era and then began quoting Leo Tolstoy and other classic Russian authors as part of his anti-colonial arguments. The majority of people in Yerevan know Russian, and whole Russian sentences will unexpectedly float up in their conversations.

— Growing up, I was taught that our most important national hero was Vasily Chapayev.

We talked about the new construction in Yerevan.

Hanging out among the artists and activists, I was told that Armenians believe that all public spaces should have owners and be developed—and that they should generate profits. Public space in Yerevan could easily become someone's private property. For example, in 2002, a millionaire named Gerard Cafesjian bought Cascade, an architectural complex that's one of the city's most recognizable symbols. One of the central parks in the city has also become private property.

—They're building goddamn churches instead of schools.

Simple Yerevanites take over city space with the methods available to them: the little gardens that abut apartment buildings are transformed into private gardens for first-floor residents. Along similar lines, it's easy to spot all the additions grafted onto building facades.

—

Yerevan is one of the most ancient cities in the world—and one of the most reconstructed.

The Blue Mosque was built during the Erivan Khanate and is now completely surrounded by residential buildings and part of the Kond neighborhood. On the territory of the Yerevan fortress and the Palace of Sardar is the headquarters of the renowned cognac manufacturer Ararat.

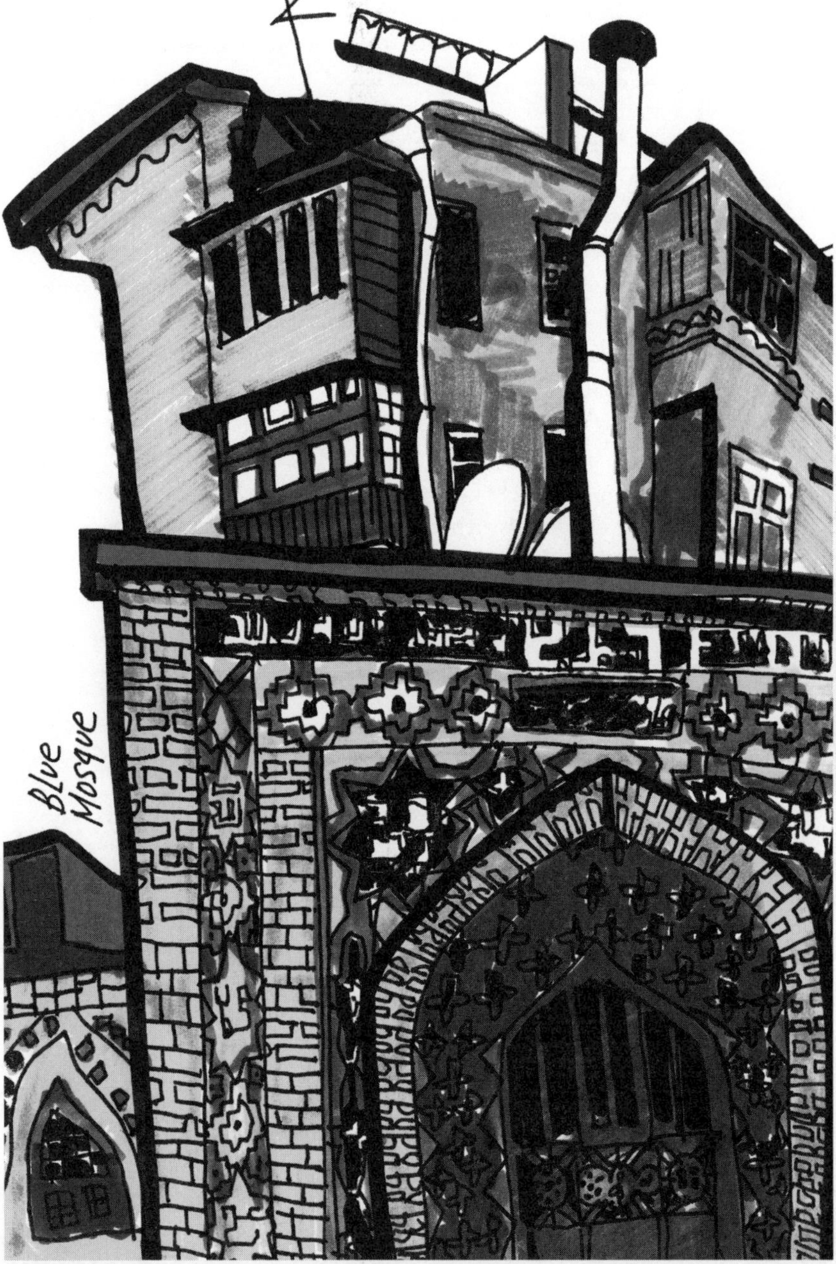
Blue Mosque

Several Iranian mosques and Armenian churches were destroyed during the Soviet era, and after the fall of the USSR, Armenians took down a number of Soviet buildings. These included the Hotel Sevan and the modernist Youth Palace, referred to by Armenians as the Corncob. All that's left of the famous Hotel Dvin is its carcass. The only reason the Moscow movie theater's avant-garde summer hall survived and wasn't replaced by a church was outcry from protesters.

Many Soviet symbols were taken down during perestroika. Lenin Square was renamed Republic Square, and the statue of Lenin by the famous sculptor Sergey Merkulov was knocked down and decapitated. My artist friends told me that this headless Lenin still lies in the inner courtyard of the National Painting Gallery. I couldn't get in there without special permission, but I could see the statue through a gallery window. Headless Lenin lay awkwardly in an empty fountain. My drawing deeply disturbed one of the visitors to the museum. "Don't show that to anybody! Don't tell anyone that *he's* lying there like that!" She couldn't explain why this was such a dangerous secret.

KOND

At the beginning of the 2000s, an entire neighborhood was demolished to make way for Northern Prospect and its elite real estate. Many residents forcibly displaced from their homes received small amounts of money for their trouble. Now Yerevan is considering doing the same with Kond, the city's oldest neighborhood.

With its prerevolutionary houses clinging to the sides of a big hill, Kond resembles an ant colony. It's easy to get lost in Kond's narrow, curving streets, many of which abruptly give way to dead ends. These houses were built and owned by the wealthy, but these days most of Kond looks more like a slum. The semi-ruins of the Iranian mosque made an especially big impression on me. Around five families have lived in it since Soviet times.

"Antique" registers as an insult in Armenian—it means something like "junk."

Many of the people who live in Kond consider it cursed, because Muslims used to own many of the houses there—Iranians, Azerbaijanis, and "Turks," which is what Azerbaijani Tatars called themselves. At the same time, the people of Kond have strong links to their community. Neighbors are very close to one another, and they have many family ties. The owner of this dovecote wanted everybody in Kond to be moved into one big, new building.

Not everybody in Kond wants to move. I went to see Nara, an activist who lives with her mother in a house her grandmother and grandfather built after they fled from Turkey during the genocide. She loves the house and wants to fix it up.

Nara told me that during the Soviet era, local authorities demanded that homeowners give up their property deeds, and that the majority of people who lived in Kond obeyed, including her grandmother. When they learned that the people whose homes were demolished during the construction of Northern Prospect found themselves thrown out in the street, the people of Kond started to worry about their future.

Nara went to all the houses in Kond, gathering her neighbors for a fight for their rights. The Kondites brought chairs to the Government House and held a sit-in demanding that their property deeds be reinstated. In the end, they succeeded.

In Armenian society, women activists are pressured through their male relatives. The protesters in Kond were all women, except for an old veteran of the Karabakh war, so the police didn't use force to disperse them. Instead, they tried to negotiate with the only man—the veteran—ignoring Nara, the leader of the movement.

— I don't have a husband, or a brother, or a son, so they can't plant guns or drugs on me.

ABOVYAN PENITENTIARY

With the support of the Rehabilitation Center for Prisoners of the Armenian Ministry of Justice, I taught a few drawing classes at the Abovyan Penitentiary. The Center provides legal and psychological support to incarcerated women and organizes regular ceramics, stained-glass, and wood engraving classes at Abovyan, the prison closest to Yerevan.

During my master classes, I met Nastya, the art star of Abovyan, who has painted several murals at the prison. She studies the paintings of Martiros Saryan and Minas Avetisyan and paints homages to their work.

There are many trees on the grounds of Abovyan, and the low walls topped with barbed wire don't fully obscure the view of the mountains. The prisoners wear their own clothes. I was told that this was because the state never designed any women's prison uniforms—"They're women, after all!"—and that conditions at women's prisons were generally less harsh than they were at men's. There are no juvenile women's prisons in Armenia; female minors are generally given probation.

A colorful crowd of women gathered in the cafeteria for lunch, carrying their own food in pots, cast-iron pans, and skillets. Almost nobody eats the prison food. Unlike Russia, where many women prisoners are cast off by their families, in Armenia, relatives take care of them throughout their incarceration.

The most common charges are fraud, drug trafficking, and sex trafficking. Armenians traffic fellow Armenians into Turkey to do sex work, because it's close and the demand is there. Women who have done time are branded for life: they have very little chance of getting regular work, building families, or even finding husbands for their daughters.

BEING AN ARMENIAN WOMAN

At one point during my visit, I was mistaken for an Armenian. I was sitting on the ground drawing a carpet seller when an elderly woman came up to me and started tugging at my skirt while lecturing me in Armenian. When she realized I was from Russia, she immediately lost interest in my morality: in Armenia, a Russian woman is a loose woman.

It's interesting to compare the pressure on women in Armenian and Russian societies. In Russia, women over 18 who are still virgins are looked down upon. Women are expected to be sexually active and to have a baby, even if that means being a single mother. In Armenia, the most important value is family honor: many women who don't get married remain "old maids" and can discuss this publicly without shame. In many Armenian marzer, or regions, the tradition of the Red Apple persists to this day: on the morning after the wedding night, the parents of the bride receive a red apple, which is meant to symbolize her virginity. It's shameful to have a child out of wedlock and shameful to get divorced. To be childless is considered a tragedy.

One day, my Armenian friend, a sociologist, came upon a bakery in a courtyard and suggested that we interview the women baking lavash. We were cheerfully invited to sit down and served coffee, but our conversation about social changes in Yerevan didn't take off. The women asked my friend how old my nonexistent children were, in Armenian, confident that I had them, and kept trying to marry her off to their sons. They only asked me one question, and once I answered it they lost all interest in carrying on our conversation.

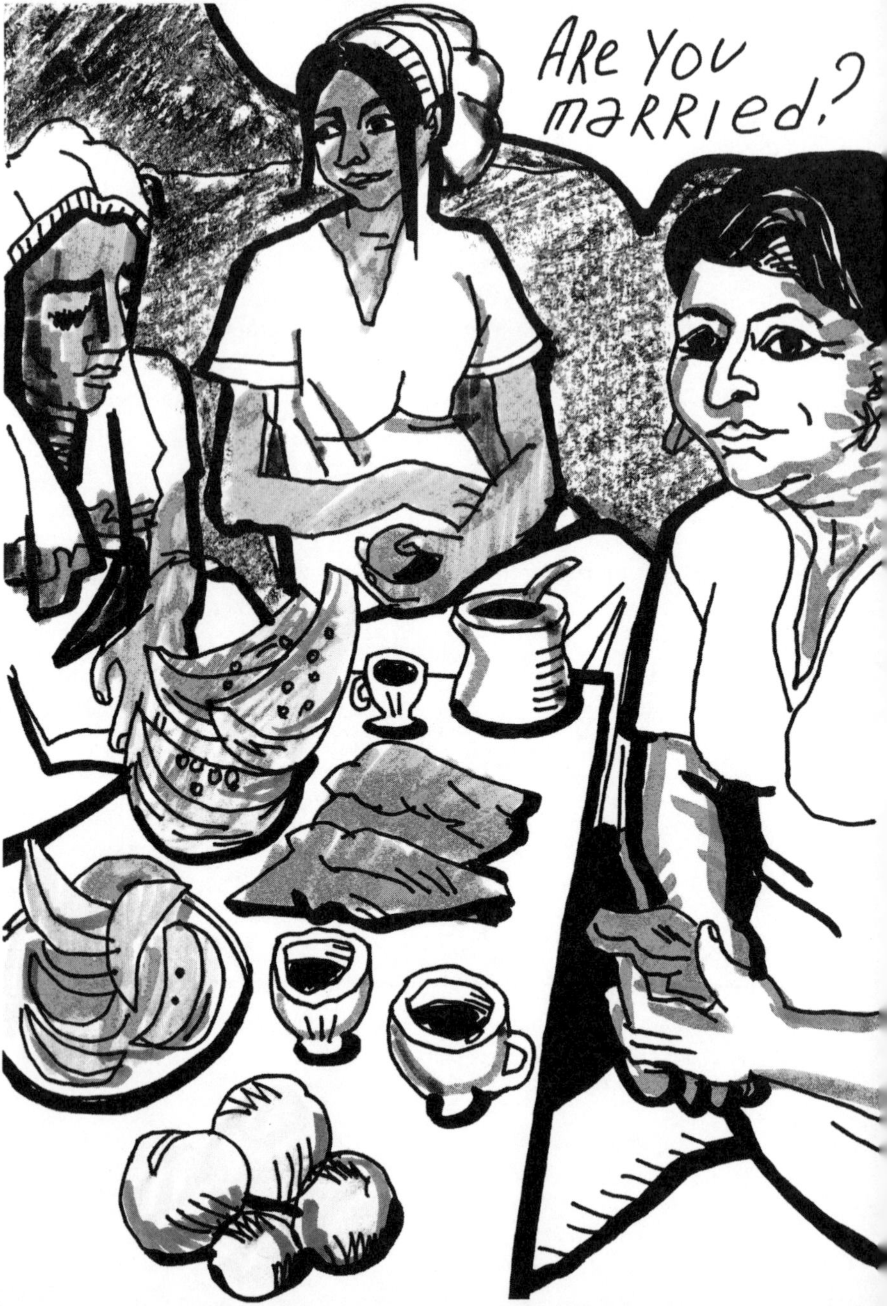
Are you married?

Domestic violence is commonplace in Armenia, just as it is in Russia. In 2010, seven women's organizations came together to form the Coalition to Stop Violence Against Women in order to lobby for a law against domestic violence and to support survivors. I went to the trial of a woman named Suzanna, whom the Coalition accompanied to court and for whom they'd found a lawyer. The woman had been beaten on a regular basis by her husband and her mother-in-law. When she filed for divorce, they took her daughter away. After the hearing, the judge demanded that the ex-spouses preserve their family and the honor of Armenian society.

> The courtroom in Vanadzor
> — A child is the light of every family. She shouldn't suffer because of her parents.

Armenia has the highest number of sex-selective abortions in the world, after China and Azerbaijan. Women usually get abortions if they already have two daughters and the third fetus is female. Unwanted daughters are sometimes named Bavakan, which means "That's Enough." A son is considered to be the continuation of the family line—a future breadwinner. A woman who gives birth to a son finds her social status rising precipitously. Traditionally, a son will bring his wife into his parents' home, and the property is left to him. A daughter is taken into her husband's family, and an unmarried woman serves her brother's family.

These kinds of patriarchal traditions are slowly coming to an end, and the young people of Yerevan are very different from their parents. This is a portrait of Arevik, a sociological researcher and feminist, with her mother, who doesn't understand why her daughter is in no rush to get married and have children.

My warmest memories of Yerevan are meeting, interviewing, and working with independent women. I think it's women like that who are helping Armenian society become softer, more flexible, and more diverse.

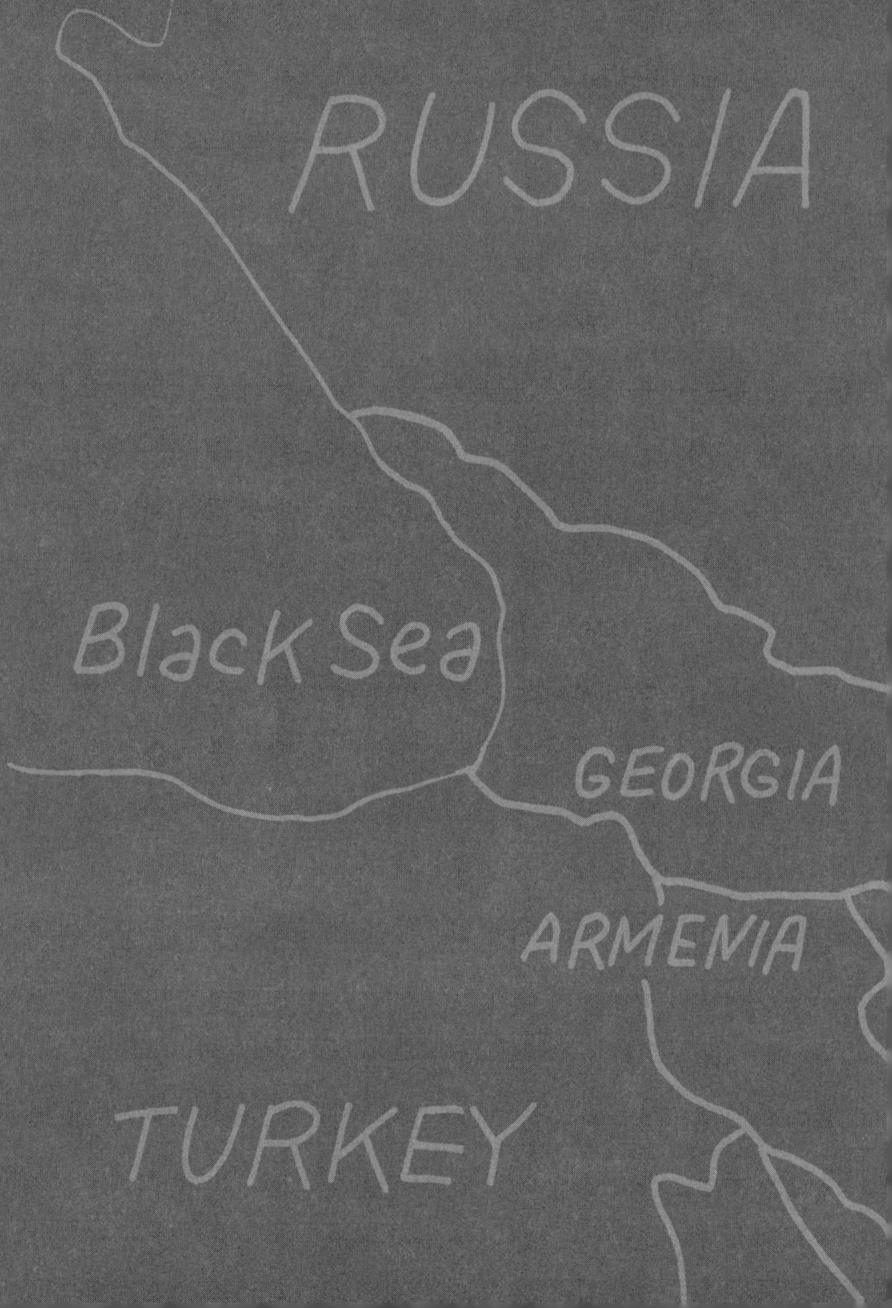
RUSSIA
Black Sea
GEORGIA
ARMENIA
TURKEY

A TRIP TO DAGESTAN, 2015

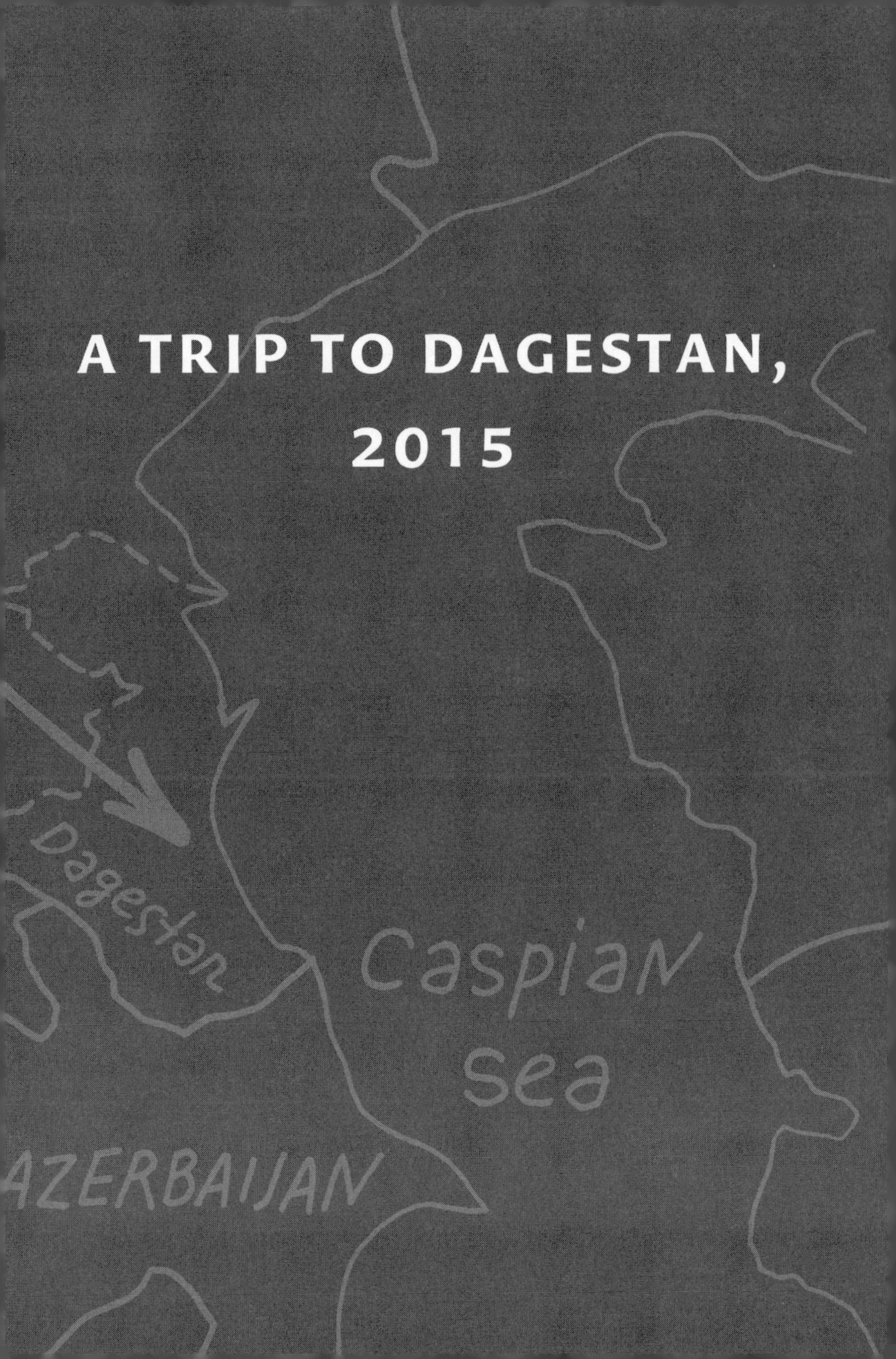
Dagestan
Caspian sea
AZERBAIJAN

MAKHACHKALA

In 2015, I was invited to give a few lectures in Makhachkala. In my free time, I explored the city. The first site I was taken to see was the prison on Scorpion Hill. "This is one of our oldest buildings," my guide told me. "It is a reconstruction of the garrison. Walls with masonry from that era have been preserved here." Another site was a regular private home from the 19th century, which is considered the most beautiful building in Makhachkala. Locals also suggested taking me around to the many markets. "Our whole city is one big bazaar," they said.

I tried to talk to people and draw them at the markets. "What's your nationality?" is a question that everybody in Makhachkala answers with pleasure. There are over thirty different nationalities in Dagestan.

Half an hour after I gave a man his free portrait, he returned with the drawing. "I took a closer look," he said, "and realized that you made the nose too big." Another model, a honey merchant, was also unsatisfied. "Everyone tells me I have a straight, Grecian nose. But in your drawing, there's a hump."

This woman asked me to do a portrait of her with her son. An elderly woman walking behind me remarked that Islam forbids depictions of people.

— Muslim women aren't supposed to let themselves be drawn. Am I committing a sin?

Students from the Dzhemal School, where I was giving my lectures, told me about people who come to study in the art department and then refuse to do figure drawing for religious reasons. "Some of the 'covered' girls destroy their figure drawings after they're done," I was told. "They only want to do costume design."

—Life drawing is prohibited by their religious beliefs.

Tatiana Borisovna, art teacher

They don't draw nude models at the art department. "In one of our classes, we once drew a guy without a shirt on," the students told me. "And even then, it happened behind closed doors. The model didn't want everyone to know he was posing for us."

This student came to my lecture on socially engaged art.

"What can a woman do in Dagestan?" Saida wondered. "Women can't dance or sing according to Islam."

Saida and Raisat are friends from Kizilyurt, a small town west of Makhachkala. They're roommates. Their families were fine with sending them off to study art, and Saida's mom even helps install her work for exhibits.

"When I was little," says Saida, "I saw a girl from a religious family in all white, with a kerchief. It was so beautiful! That was the first time I asked my mother to get me a kerchief like that. When I started reading the Koran, I understood that I was wearing the kerchief for myself. Anyone could go up to an uncovered girl and ask for her phone number. I like wearing a hijab, a tunic, and jeans."

If anyone objects to me drawing, I'm gonna get mad.

Saida and Raisat, students

"I want to wear a kerchief," says Madina, a student, "but if I did my parents would think I'd been recruited by the Wahhabis. I know someone whose husband was recruited—they moved to Syria with their children. They're certain that if they die there, they'll go straight to heaven. There are girls who take off their kerchiefs when they leave their house, and others who put on their kerchiefs when their parents aren't looking."

People try to marry girls off as soon as they can, before they start forming their own opinions.

Uma

"As soon as they can" means before they turn 20. In Dagestan, it's important for a husband to be able to easily train a woman to be a good wife.

Uma's mother is a music teacher, and her father is an artist. "When I said that I wanted to go to school to become an artist," she said, "my father silently left the room. He came back in with a sketchbook."

I noticed many attractive women in Makhachkala. I tried to meet one of these "bombits"—a local subculture of fashionable women with long black hair and lip fillers—but ended up meeting a model.

Though she was still a very young woman, the model had already gotten married, dealt with domestic violence at home, and gotten divorced. There's no name on this drawing because there are only a handful of models in Dagestan. "Being a model here is risky," she said. "I don't go out in the street."

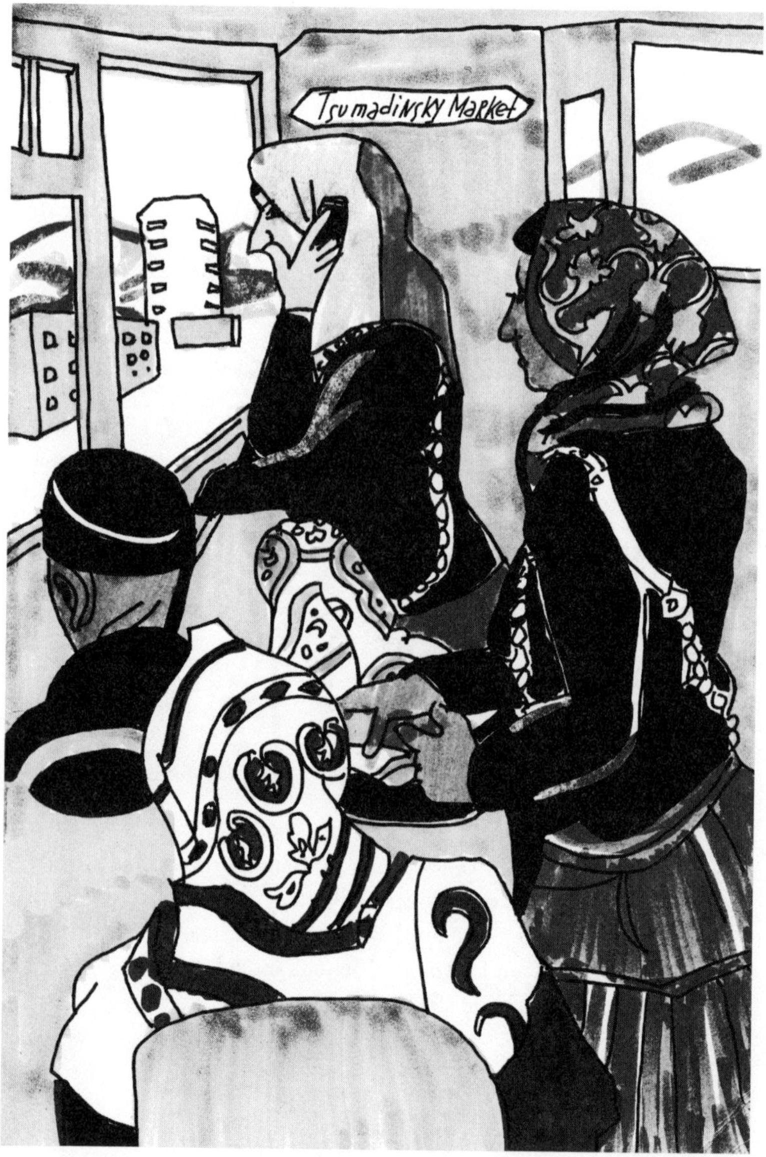
Tsumadinsky Market

HIGH MOUNTAIN VILLAGES:
KIDERO, MOKOK, BEZHTA

In Makhachkala, I met an ethnographer named Patimat Magomedova. Patia invited me to join her on a trip to the high mountain villages on the border with Georgia. She was doing field work about female circumcision in Dagestan. In Kidero, she interviewed a woman who had been performing these operations for many years.

> I do it the way my stepmother taught me. I tell everyone that I can teach them. One nurse wanted to learn, but how was I supposed to just show her? Bring me a girl.

"I cut off a tiny dot so that it bleeds. All you need is a small drop of blood. We did circumcisions in Soviet times, too. I get the girls before they start their periods. Afterwards they get too embarrassed, and I'm embarrassed to look, too. When I got mine, the girl ahead of me, who was older, started screaming that it hurt. I ran away—my grandma had to come catch me. Afterwards, she told me, 'Now you'll be beautiful. You'll start doing the Salah. You'll do well in school.'"

Why do people do these circumcisions? Some women said, "We got them, so we will give them to our daughters." Others said that this practice followed from the Sunnah. "Muhammed did it to his daughters," I was told, "and so all Muslim women have to do it." But most of them were going to get their daughters circumcised, or had already done so, so that girls "wouldn't go messing around."

Mothers make the decision regarding their daughters' circumcisions, with the fathers' passive approval. Some decide to do it even in spite of their husbands' objections. "Times are hard," I heard. "There are a lot of women and not many men. A girl needs to be circumcised, so that she can live on her own if she needs to."

In Kidero, we stayed with a relative of Patimat's named Bika. Bika is her husband's second wife. This is common in Dagestan: Bika's husband lives in another village with his first wife, and from time to time he comes to stay with Bika.

"After I got divorced, I was alone with two kids, but still, I didn't want to become a second wife," Bika said. "When my current husband began courting me, my relatives noticed, and that's when the gossip began. Like it or not, I had to say yes. Now things are good. It's just too hard to be a divorced woman in the village. Even if you're on perfect behavior, people will start to talk."

Bika also told this story: "There was a shootout in Kidero one time, and two cops were killed. Later on, some of the women started arguing about second wives. The widow of one of the cops heard them and said, 'I wouldn't mind it if my husband had had even nine if that meant he would still be alive. At least that way I could see him, even just once a year.' After that, everybody fell into an awkward silence."

"A second wife is a sanctioned lover," said Patimat. According to her, nobody stays with their second wives into their old age. According to Islam, men are supposed to provide equally for both wives, but second wives often don't receive meaningful financial support.

Here is what Patimat thought about a Chechnyan wedding that made international headlines, in which a 46-year-old Kadyrovite named Nazhud Guchigov married a 17-year-old girl.

"I don't understand why this marriage in particular caused so much scandal—you even see 14-year-old brides sometimes. A girl forced into marriage—that happens all the time, too. And often parents really do know best. I wouldn't want my life discussed in such a public way. I thought the Chechens were going to murder the journalist who wrote about the story."

At another house:

"Why are there only women here?"

"She's a second wife, her husband doesn't live with her, so the only men who can come over are her male relatives."

In Kidero, I met with Sirajuddin Abdurakhmanov, the author of *On the Hairpin Curves of Our Lives*, a book about the forced resettlement of Dagestanis to Chechnya in 1944, and then back to Dagestan between 1956 and 1958.

"They resettled a few areas, but the only one they razed completely was ours, the Tsuntinsky region," said Abdurakhmanov. "They burned down homes right in front of the residents, because they refused to leave. Families lost five to six people on the way there, or in Chechnya. A lot of people came down with malaria, it was a harsh adjustment. The Chechens—they tried to give Hitler a horse with a golden saddle. But us? What did we get deported for?"

Abdurakhmanov was born in Chechnya and finished sixth grade there. I asked him what he remembered about returning to Kidero. "We went back to the mountains on ZILs. One vehicle per household, we had to leave a lot behind. When the road ended, we had to walk the rest of the way."

> My parents returned to find that there was no house anymore. They were told that they had to get the kolkhoz back up and running first. Then they could worry about themselves.
>
> — Sirajuddin Abdurakhmanov

When I asked why Abdurakhmanov described the Stalin era as "just and caring" in his book, he was offended. "Could Stalin have seen what the deportation looked like on the ground?" he asked. "What do you think he was busy doing during the war?"

For years now, Abdurakhmanov and others have been advocating for the official recognition of the deportation of Dagestanis as a historical fact. They want the people from the Tsuntinsky region, whose homes were burned down, to be compensated for their losses. He believes that the most important thing is to "get it on Putin's desk." When he learned that a Muscovite interested in local history had come to Kidero, he walked across the village in the rain to meet me. He was visibly disappointed by the fact that, although I work in Moscow, I don't have any connections to the President.

— Why isn't there anything in the Russian textbooks about the forced deportation of Dagestanis?

The people in the neighboring village of Mokok are also hoping for help from Moscow. Their school is crumbling, the walls may cave in on the kids at any moment. They've been demanding repairs for twenty years. Officials from Makhachkala came to town, there were articles in the Dagestani press, but none of that did anything.

"They're offering to shut down our school and bus our kids to the next village over," the elementary school teacher told me. "But our roads are too dangerous."

This is gym class. "The girls do their push-ups at home," the teacher said. "The boys do their push-ups here, on the floor, because we don't have any mats."

The school is heated with firewood, and classes are regularly interrupted because of the smoke. Beginning in October, the children sit in class with their coats on. "Our ruin of a school is in first place in all the regional competitions," the principal told me. "These desks have been here since I was a student here. We only do cosmetic repairs."

There's no good road to Mokok. When there is snow or rain or ice, the narrow mountain road leading to the village becomes treacherous and unpassable. Villagers—especially the women—leave very rarely. Life is more isolated here than in the neighboring villages. Perhaps this is why many of the marriages here are between close relatives. A woman who married her cousin explained, "How could you just marry some stranger?"

Patimat and I visited a large family. The couple had ten adult children, thirty grandchildren, and two great-granddaughters. All the children except for the youngest son live independently, in their own homes. The son's parents hope that he'll get married soon, but that he'll keep living with them, so that their daughter-in-law can help them around the house.

> When my wife was pregnant with our last child, the doctor said she might die—she needed to get an abortion. I told him, "Let her die. I'm not going to kill my own children."

The majority of men are on social media, but they don't let their wives partake. As in the rest of Dagestan, women are under the authority of their fathers and brothers and male cousins, and then their husbands. "God forbid my sister starts talking to some guy on the phone!" the youngest brother said. "I'd be ashamed in front of the whole village."

The last place we visited was Bezhta, Patimat's home village. Everybody I talked to from there told me that they had an "enlightened society" in the village. They see places like Kidero and Mokok as being overly religious. In Soviet times, people from Bezhta would often travel to Georgia, and many of them still have a fondness for Georgian culture.

I asked Patimat's great-uncle, who'd been a teacher at the village school in Soviet times, how communist ideology, Islam, and mountain laws all worked together.

He told me that it had been forbidden to pray openly, but everyone prayed at home. Teachers made sure students didn't pray in school. Girls came to school in their Young Pioneers ties and their headscarves. One woman from Bezhta remembered how in the '80s, there were a few years of campaigns against this—the authorities tried to make girls keep their heads uncovered in class.

The teacher noticed his future wife in school and asked her parents for her hand.

It was considered shameful to spend time together before marriage. It wasn't until the '60s or '80s—different people said different things—that young people began to meet one another on their own and socialize before getting married. "It's better the way it is now," Patimat's aunts said.

"If the relationships between men and women were totally dictated by mountain customs, how was the Soviet ideology of gender equality expressed?" I asked.

"They sat boys and girls at the same desks in school," Patimat's relatives responded.

This is how evening get-togethers look in Bezhta. There's wi-fi in every home and most people use social media. Children are glued to TVs and have begun speaking to one another in Russian. The older population learned Russian in school, but only spoke Bezhta in their daily lives.

Women on head coverings:

In Kidero: "If I start walking around uncovered, my relatives will kill me."

In Mokok: "They cover girls' heads when they're between 3 and 5. People are already grumbling about my daughter going around uncovered, but if I could I'd avoid putting a kerchief on her until she was 10."

In Bezhta: "You can wear whatever you like here—even a kimono."

Despite the "enlightened" nature of the village, there has never been a dance club here. The locals believe that kind of place is for "women of loose behavior." People most often meet at weddings. It's still crucial to remain a virgin before marriage. "If you have premarital sex," I was told, "the guy won't marry you." Bezhta women were very surprised when I told them that in Russia people live together before getting married.

I took a taxi-bus back to Makhachkala, which took almost seven hours. While we all shook as the bus made its way over terrifying turns that looked out onto sharp drop-offs, a fellow rider told me about how they used to go to the city in Soviet times. "Even in winter, it'd be in the open back of a truck, wrapped in a blanket. It's a lot more comfortable now." The taxi-bus runs from Bezhta to Makhachkala every morning. From Kidero it runs once a week, and from Mokok you need to take your own car.

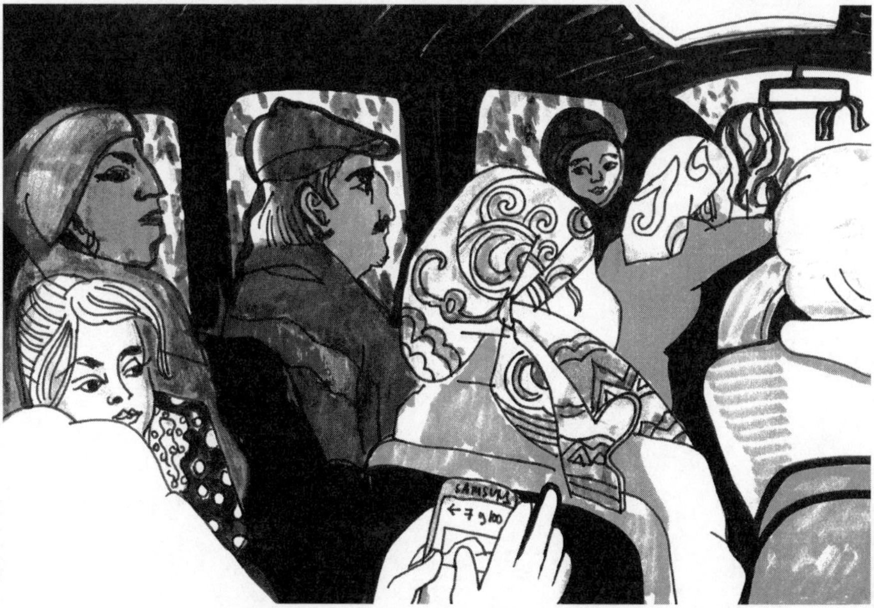

UKRAINE
Sea of AZOV
RUSSIA
Black Sea
GEORGIA
Tbilisi
ARMENIA
TURKEY

TRAVELS TO TBILISI, 2015–16

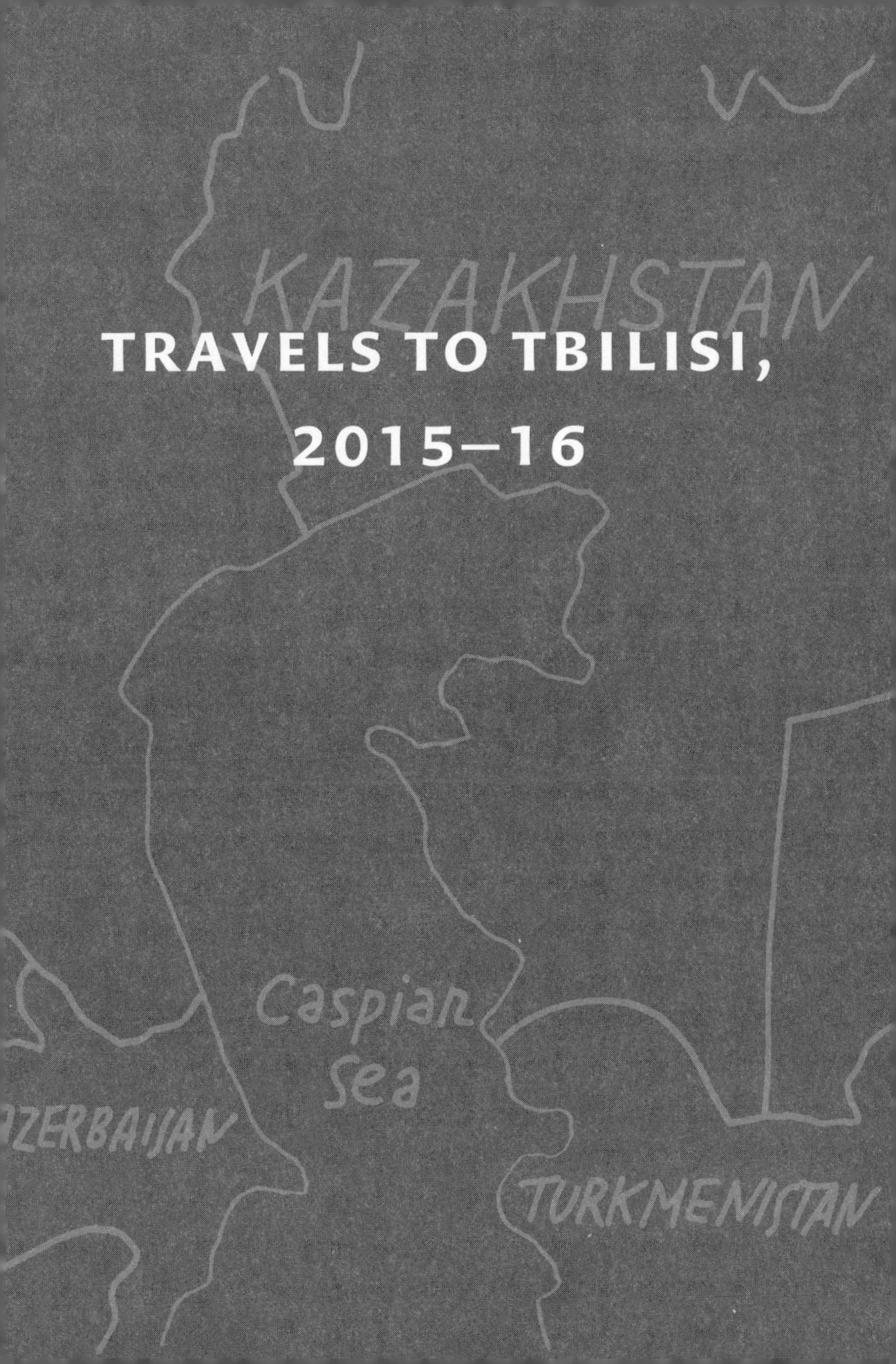
KAZAKHSTAN
Caspian
Sea
ZERBAIJAN
TURKMENISTAN

APRIL 9

Even before my first trip to Tbilisi, I'd heard a lot of great things about the city from friends. They told me about the beauty and hospitality of the Georgians, about long meals full of song, about Tbilisi's ancient courtyards.... I wondered what new things I could possibly have to say about such a touristy place.

In the very first Tbilisi home I visited, I heard about April 9, 1989. The owners of the house were surprised that this date didn't mean anything to me—for them, as for many Georgians, this was the critical turning point in Russian–Georgian relations. I decided to talk to people who'd participated in the events of that day.

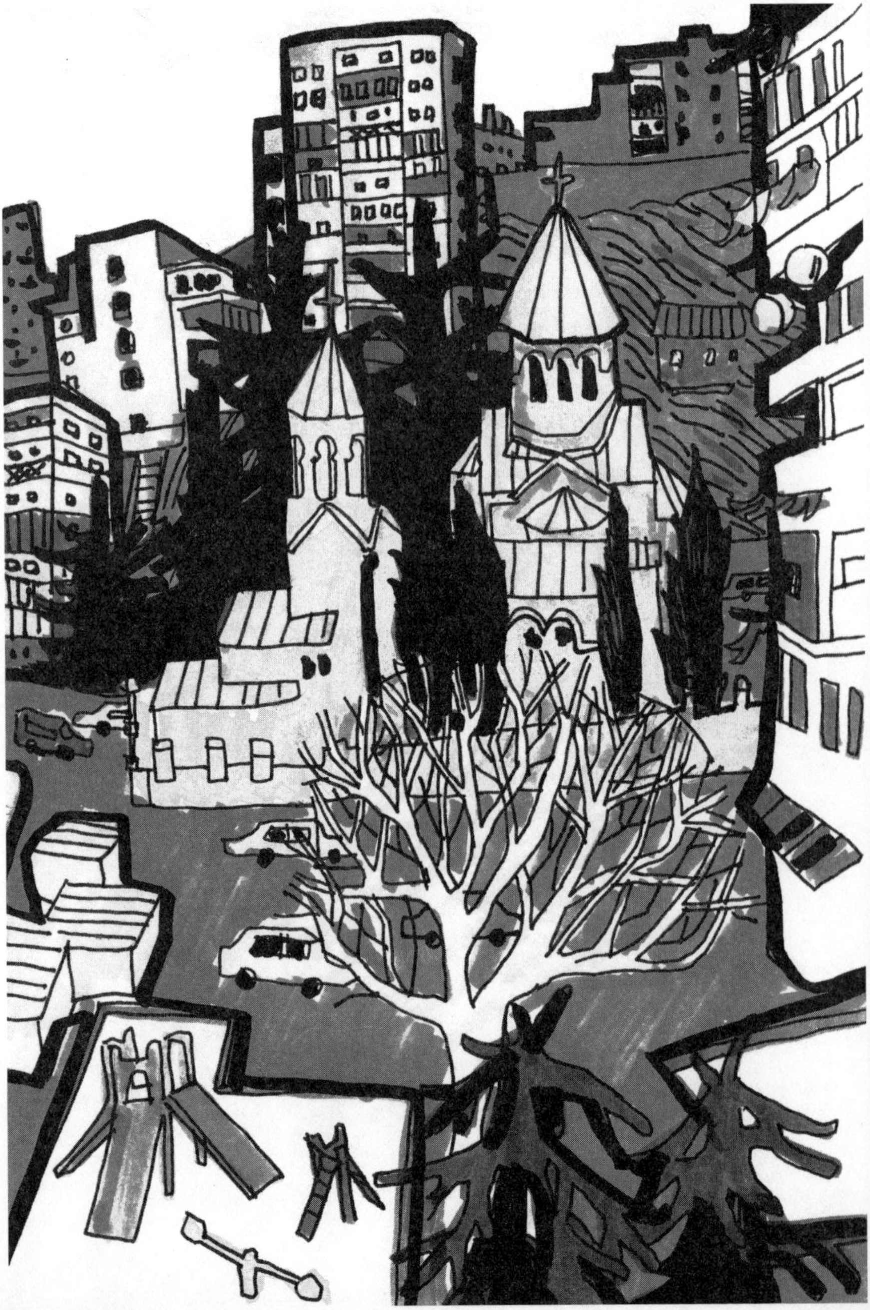

"April 9 turned everything on its head," said Nukry, a driver who'd demonstrated for Georgian independence in 1989. "People were beaten with shovels, like livestock. If they'd just shot at us, at least we've been through that before." Some of the shovels Soviet soldiers used to beat peaceful demonstrators are on display at Tbilisi's Museum of the Soviet Occupation.

The demonstrations began in Tbilisi on April 2. On April 7 and 8, tanks and army battalions entered the city. Many people realized that they would be forcibly dispersed. Catholicos-Patriarch Ilia II called on the demonstrators to come pray at the churches instead, but they didn't listen. Minutes later, soldiers attacked the crowd using shovels and toxic gas. Several people were killed, mostly women.

> The tanks cleared the way for the troops. People started tearing up the sidewalk and throwing the slabs at the soldiers. We weren't scared — we were angry.

Eka, director of Women's Initiatives Supporting Group (WISG), a feminist organization, participated in the 1989 demonstrations with her friends from college. "Somebody with a bullhorn announced that tanks and soldiers had entered the city, so we sat down in the street. We wanted to block the road."

> I remember the face of the soldier in front of me, his narrow eyes full of hate. The soldiers were agitated, they couldn't wait to attack us.

"The Georgian police tried to defend us," Eka recalled. "They'd been disarmed ahead of time, but they formed a human shield in front of us. We were kettled into the Rustaveli movie theater, where we found an emergency exit and fled. They killed sixteen people. We felt despair, but not powerlessness. We threw rocks at the tanks."

Mikhail Gorbachev refused to take responsibility for these events. At first, officials tried to claim that people had died in a stampede.

"I hate big governments," said Nukri. "I want all big governments to get broken up into lots of tiny pieces and never get the chance to do these kinds of things to smaller states."

The journalist Gala Petri moved to Tbilisi from Irkutsk in 1984. She remembers how, at the end of the '80s and beginning of the '90s, "there was a lot of primitive patriotism going around." Before April 9, the Georgian elite had spoken Russian and it had been fashionable to send kids to Russian schools, but afterwards, people began disparaging those same kids. Gala transferred her daughter to a Georgian school. She doesn't recall there being any kind of physical violence toward Russians. "Russians left Georgia after that, but it was for economic reasons," she said.

When I got back to Moscow, I asked many friends and acquaintances about what they knew about the tragic events of April 9. Only one person was able to give me an answer—Israpil Shovkhalov, editor of *Dosh*, the independent Caucasian magazine. In 1989, he served for a year in Samtredia, a town in western Georgia.

"On April 9," Israpil told me, "I was on patrol along with the other soldiers. People were gathering on the streets, talking to one another in Georgian. They were worried. In the evening a rumor had made its way to town that in Tbilisi, soldiers had killed a pregnant woman with a shovel in the midst of keeping the protests down. Before April 9 the people in town had been kind—they fed the soldiers for free—but after that they started to treat us like killers."

"One day, the soldiers from Tbilisi who had dispersed the demonstration came to our base. They told us that Georgians were really brave and brazen—they'd come at them with just their bare hands and fight, both the men and the women. Not all the soldiers were ready to use shovels and gas on the protestors. So they got beaten up."

When I quit, all I could think about was how I was going to get home alive. That was the atmosphere. On the train, I told everyone I was a Chechen. That softened them up a bit.

RELIGIOSITY

Eka and Natia, the co-director of WISG, were among the activists who held a LGBT rally in downtown Tbilisi in 2013. On May 17, the hundred or so pro-LGBT demonstrators were met by a mob of twenty to thirty thousand people, with a group of priests at the head of the crowd. The police lost control of the flow of people and began evacuating the LGBT activists in buses and vans. Many of them were seriously injured. Only four of the attackers were issued fines, for 100 lari (less than 40 euros).

"There were five of us on that bus, and the crowd chased after us," Natia said. "The majority of the attackers were men between 17 and 40. I thought that if they managed to reach us, they would rape us right there, in public, and then kill us. Not a single one of the windows in our van remained intact. Three people got concussions. I couldn't ride public transportation for a long time after that. I was always trying to figure out who had thrown rocks at me."

Nino, another journalist, also has a clear memory of the events of May 17. She was covering the rally for a magazine called *Liberali*, and she was also there as an ally. She had come with a gay male journalist. Her friends gave her a poster that read "I have the right to love." Nino remembers that when the attack began, she threw her poster down. All she could think about was how to make it out alive and get her gay colleague out with her.

Several days after our conversation, Nino wrote me to tell me that her 17-year-old son, a stylish young man with long hair, had been beaten up on the street by a group of guys who thought he was gay. He'd been on the phone with his girlfriend and, before hanging up, had said "Love you!" That's when he was attacked. "How dare you, faggot!" they yelled at him.

This piece is from my master class on feminist stencils on paper, which I led for Georgian activists in Tbilisi.

THINK OUTSIDE THE CROSS

The stool is almost symbolic: one of the priests attacking the LGBT demonstrators on May 17 had used a stool as a weapon.

The main topic that the master class participants wanted to explore was the way that society, the family, and the church attempt to control female sexuality. They talked about how hard it is for young, sexually active, unmarried women to get gynecological services. "It's Google instead of gynecologists," I was told, "and priests instead of therapists."

Religious Georgians don't only want control over women's behavior. In 2015, an organizer of an activist library was attacked by a group of young men from the neighborhood. They showed up during a lecture on *Thus Spoke Zarathustra*, and one of them didn't like the line "God is dead." "Some lowlife tough guy showed up, asked who had organized the lecture, and then stuck a knife in my heart," said Mikhail, who miraculously survived. After he got out of the hospital, he moved the library to another location, where he continued his lecture series.

Some Georgian artists try to criticize the church. The activist Irakli, on a 2015 protest:

The church here eats up 25 million Lari. On the patriarch's birthday, some artists wrote "25,000,000" on the sidewalk in front of the patriarchate. They were summoned by the police the following day.

Religious Georgians were outraged by the artist Lia Ukleba's painting *The Virgin with a Toy Pistol*. The painting depicts the Virgin Mary holding a gun to her head. Despite the great influence of the church, the artist managed to suffer nothing worse than online attacks. In Georgia there are no laws like we have in Russia, for "inciting hatred or enmity" or "insulting the religious feelings of believers."

There are a lot of newly built churches in Tbilisi, especially in the Saburtalo district. For example, this church, erected on Panaskertel-Tsitsishvili Street in 2003, sits on a lot seized from a state-funded preschool.

"Why didn't anyone protest when they took away a huge part of the preschool's property?" I asked a Georgian friend who lives on that street. She explained that the people who lived in the district would have been the ones to attack any activists who spoke out against building a church.

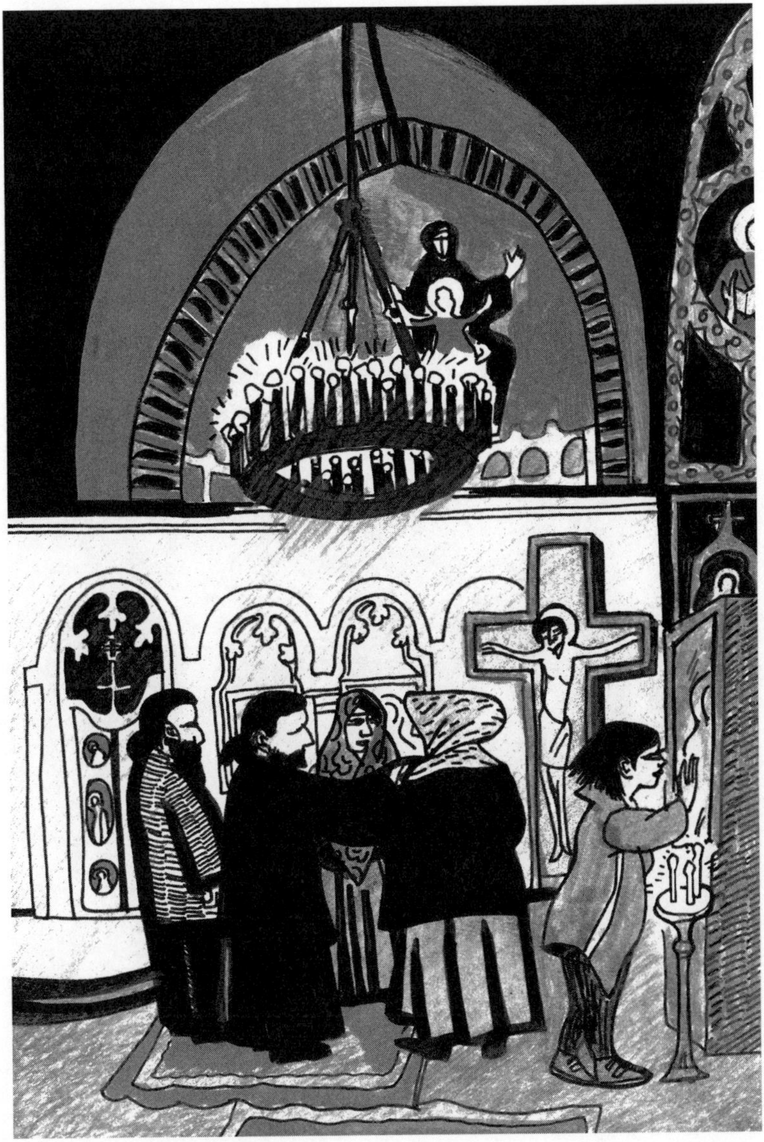

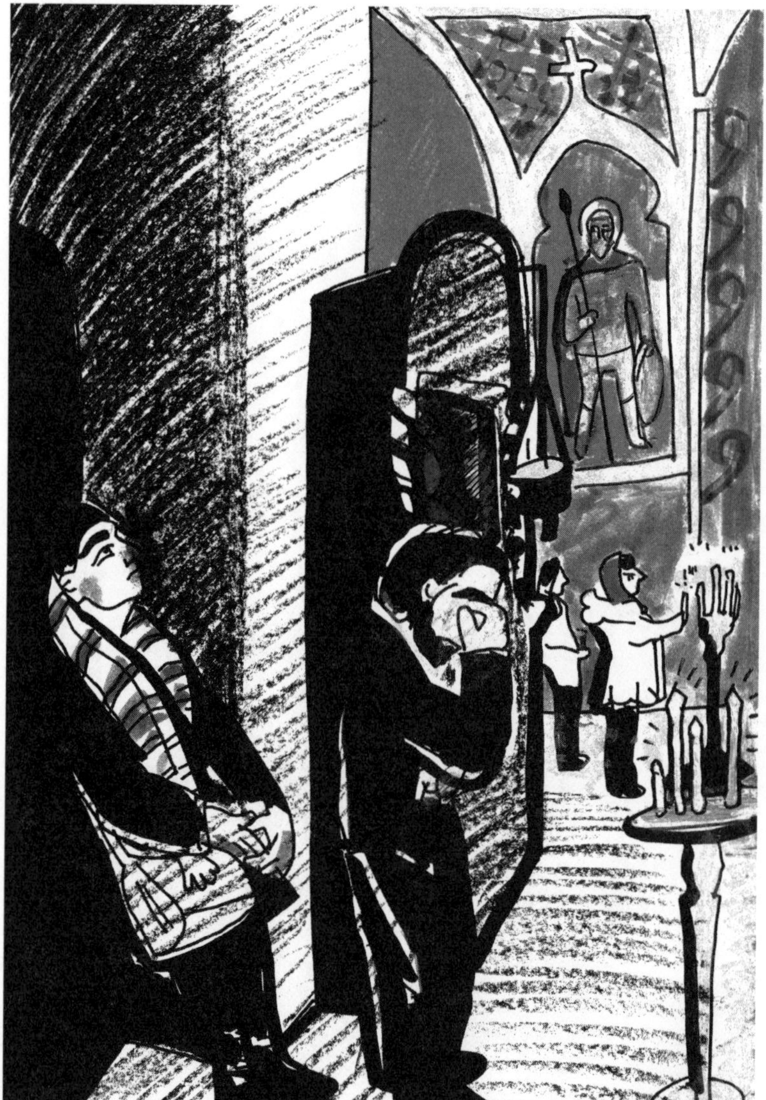

Unlike in Moscow, churches in Tbilisi don't resemble government buildings with priests who act like bureaucrats. There are pews around the entire perimeter of the church; whoever wants to can sit during services, not just the elderly and the ill. No one forbid me from drawing. I noticed that some women were wearing jeans and no head coverings. Congregants chatted with the priest before and after the service.

Georgia didn't stop being religious in Soviet times. Most of the elderly people I talked to, including the ideologically committed communists, said that they had been faithful and gone to church in the USSR.

My friends in Tbilisi told me that I should talk to Father Guram, a more liberal priest. Here is a fragment of our conversation:

"Does the Georgian church help the homeless, the poor, and the struggling?"

"Unlike the Catholic church, the Orthodox church is more about mysticism and the Gospels than it is a charitable organization."

"What can you say about the attack on the 2013 LGBT rally that was led by priests?"

"Georgians are a hot-blooded people—somebody could have been killed. But we still had the right to nonviolent protest. How could a traditional country like ours take something like this lying down? Even in Europe it's not easy."

I told Father Guram that in 2008, I had drawn the trial surrounding the Forbidden Art show in Moscow, which had been instigated by Orthodox activists in Moscow. I told him about the way they had threatened and insulted me, about how after that trial, I developed an aversion to the church. When I finished my story, he suddenly hugged me and kissed me, anointed me with his miter, and asked me to wait a minute. He left the room and came back with a bouquet of violets.

NOT FOR TOURISTS

There are people asking for money on every corner in downtown Tbilisi. Roma women with children, old people, the homeless. In addition to the refugees from Abkhazia and the Tskhinvali region (part of which is now considered Southern Ossetia), some of whom still live in former dormitories and barracks housing, there are a lot of internal migrants in Tbilisi who move to the capital to escape the hard life in the countryside. The homeless include people who didn't manage to pay off their loans or were swindled when buying an apartment.

The homeless squat in old buildings abandoned since the fall of the Soviet Union. There are nearly four hundred squats in the city. The government forces people who live there to choose between moving out or not receiving welfare. In some cases, however, the buildings have been recognized as official, legal residences.

A sociologist from a human rights organization that conducts field studies took me along to one of the biggest squats. People moved into the building, once a former hospital and cardiological institute, in 2012.

Among the squatters, there were people with college degrees who had once had careers in their fields and rented their homes. At some point, they lost their jobs and found themselves on the streets. According to the official statistics, unemployment in Georgia is at 12 percent, but a study by the National Democratic Institute (NDI) revealed that it was over 50 percent.

The homeless have limited contacts and opportunities. Mostly, they marry one another. I saw a lot of little kids who had been born in the squat.

The women didn't speak Russian. The sociologist told me that some of them said that they had left their homes because of domestic violence. Only one young man spoke Russian to me—he'd lived for a few years in St. Petersburg and had even done time in a Russian prison. "I fucked around a lot," he said, "girls, heroin . . ."

Water is brought in with buckets—there's a free tap in the courtyard of the squat. The residents steal electricity by hooking up wires to the street lights. The police regularly cut those wires. Sewage goes into the building basement. For heat, they have their cast-iron stoves.

Heating isn't just a problem in squats. Tbilisi's central heating system broke down in 1991, during the civil war. In those years of poverty, people dug up the pipes and sold off the metal for scrap. New buildings have their own heating systems, and those who live in old buildings use space heaters.

FOR TOURISTS

In the old city of Tbilisi, there are entire blocks in catastrophic states of disrepair. Only a fraction of the facades was restored under President Mikheil Saakashvili.

A strange glass and metal edifice soars over the ancient, ramshackle buildings on Sololaki Hill. This is the residence and business center of the former prime minister and billionaire Bidzina Ivanishvili. When I tried to get close to the complex through the botanical garden, a security guard came out of the bushes and told me that I was about to trespass onto private property.

The security guard's name was Georgy. He told me that he'd moved here from Gori because there was no work there. He'd been a construction worker on the complex and was kept on to do security.

"Construction began in 2001, and it was intense," said Georgy. "The modern business center opened in 2008. The Leghvtakhevi gorge is nearby. There's really beautiful nature and clean air. The business center has its own gorge and a grand oval hall."

While we were talking, a waterfall suddenly started pouring out of the cliff. It turned out that both the cliff and the waterfall were artificial—the owner could turn it on and off.

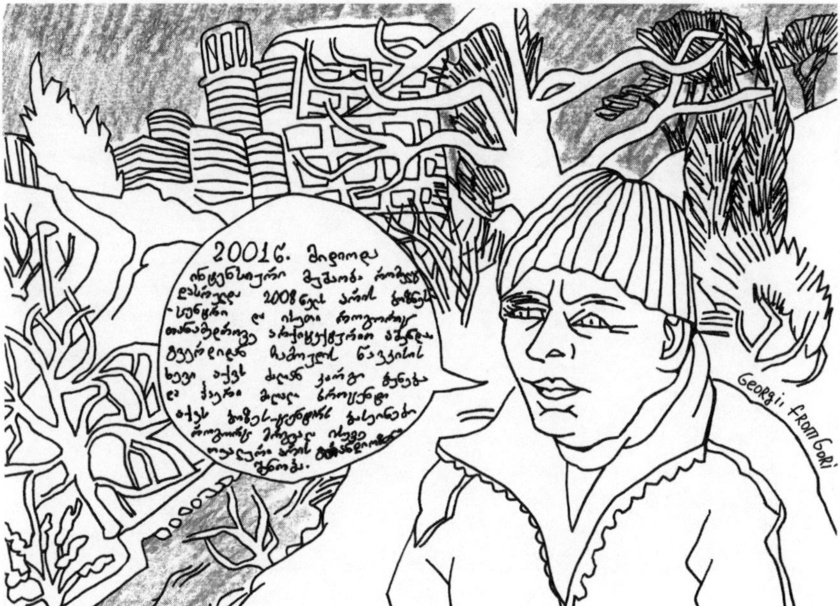
GEORGII FROM GORI

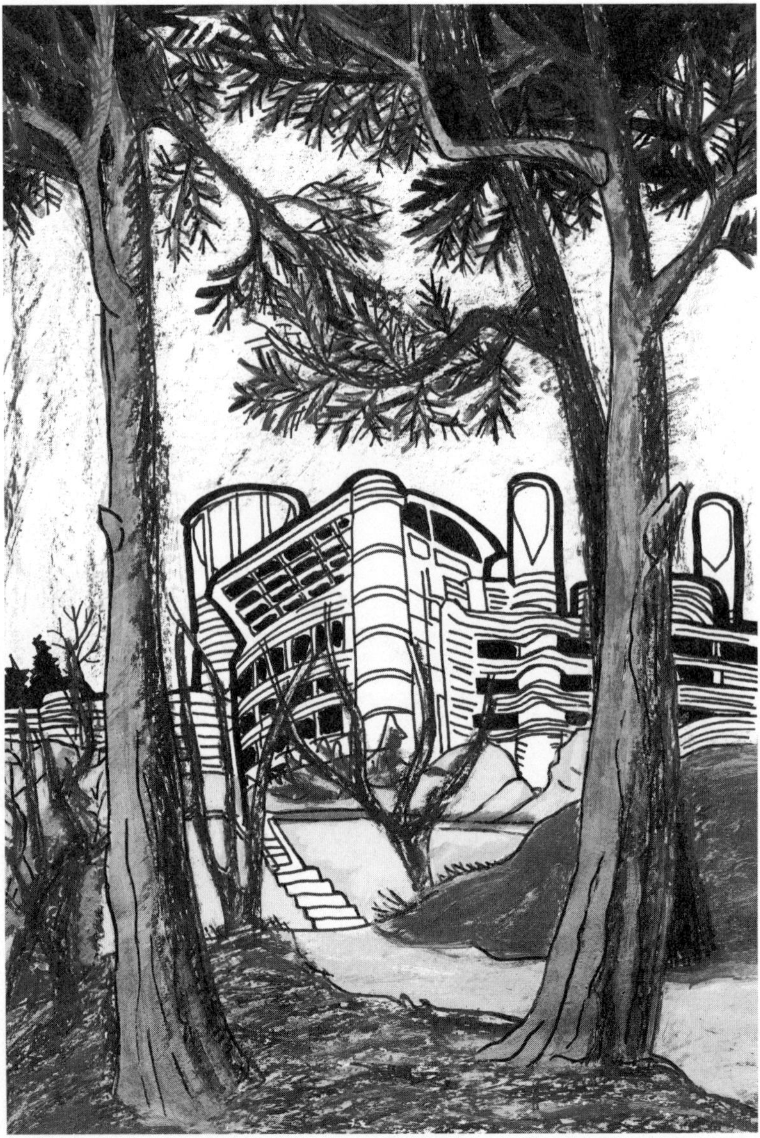

Plans are in the works for a giant, high-tech tourist complex on Bidzin Ivanishvili's Sololaki Hill. Three more complexes with hotels and business centers are being planned for other historic districts of Tbilisi. The project is called Panorama Tbilisi, and Ivanishvili believes it will attract more tourism to the city. The project's opponents believe that it will deface the city.

On February 27, I went to a protest against the new construction. It was attended by a handful of NGOs, architects and historic preservationists, environmental activists, feminists, animal rights activists, a bike advocacy group, and people from other civic initiatives. The young people—members of the so-called Saakashvili generation—looked stylish and self-assured, and many had brought their small children.

Despite the considerable size of the protest, it was completely ignored by the government. Construction has already begun in several parts of the city.

THE SOVIET PAST

Almost all Soviet symbolism has been taken down across Tbilisi, which is why I was surprised to find a Soviet military monument two steps away from Rustaveli Avenue, in what is now called April 9 Park.

It turned out that the monument had been erected in honor of Georgia's incorporation into the USSR. Its title, "Let the Banners Wave on High!", is a reference to a poem by Galaktion Tabidze:

> Day's breaking! The hot, flaming
> Sphere is rising from the sea ...
> Let the banners wave on high!
> The soul hungers to be free

One of my friends explained that Tabidze wrote the poem in 1918, when Georgia declared itself an independent nation, but that in Soviet times, they changed the date ascribed to the poem to 1921: "the year Georgia was occupied by Bolsheviks."

"Let the Banners Wave on High!"

In Tbilisi you can visit Stalin's Underground Printing House Museum, which sits behind red gates adorned with golden stars and hammers and sickles. The printing house was in operation from 1903 to 1906. Georgian social democrats, including a young Iosif Dzhugashvili, would enter the underground space through a tunnel in a well. This was where they would print revolutionary leaflets and newspapers on German presses.

The museum has no cash register, no schedule, no workers. Tours are led by an elderly Georgian man named Soso. He introduced himself as a former lieutenant in the KGB. He said that when he returned to Tbilisi from Moscow after the fall of the USSR, he wasn't able to get a pension or an apartment, so he moved into the museum and now survives on donations. "Sometimes, no one will come for two weeks at a time!" he complained.

While I was talking to Soso, some children from the neighborhood ran in. They said that this was the first time they'd ever seen the gates open and they wanted to see what was inside. They started looking at all the portraits and busts of Stalin and Lenin. "Do you know who that is?" I asked them, pointing at a Lenin. They didn't.

As we parted ways, Soso said I should stop by a garden and museum commemorating Stalin, which was built and run by an ex-taxi driver in the inner courtyard of his apartment building.

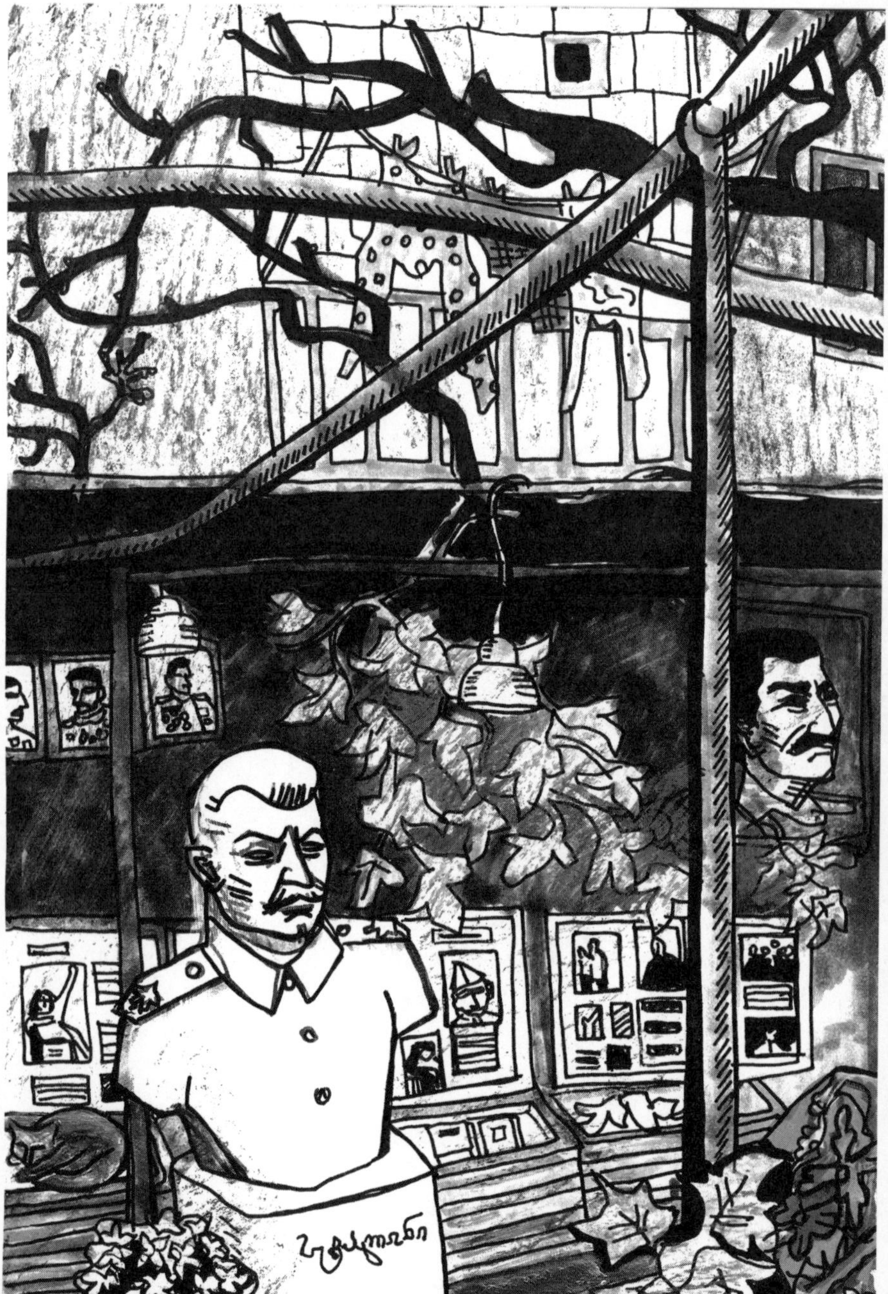
სტალინი

Ushangi Davidovich, the one-time former taxi driver, is 86. When I asked him about the Stalin era, he recalled how every year the grocery prices would go down, and pointed out the showcases around his garden that contained printouts of Stalin-era prices for all kinds of goods.

Ushangi Davidovich built his museum alone. Over time he bought up historical photographs, portraits, and busts, and he built the model of Stalin's house in Gori with his own hands. He brought back Soviet Army helmets and grenade shards from outside Stalingrad. There's a stele in the museum in memory of his son, and an ancient photograph of his parents sits next to a photo of Stalin at a parade. The walls are decorated with garlands of garlic, dried fruit, and flowers.

The wall where the museum exhibit begins is covered in framed black-and-white photographs. The faces in them are young and attractive. These are the participants of a 1956 demonstration, who were executed for their involvement.

After the XX Congress of the Communist Party at which Khrushchev spoke out against Stalin, there was a panic in Tbilisi. "There were rallies by Stalin's monument every day," Ushangi Davidovich recalled. "We demanded an explanation. On March 9, Khrushchev ordered the troops to open fire on us. The shooting began without any warning. I had stepped away to get something to eat—that's why I'm alive. They killed twenty-seven people, the youngest of whom was 15. There's nothing about any of this in the history books." Immediately afterward, Ushangi Davidovich began creating his Stalin museum.

Ushangi invited me into his home to warm up with homemade chacha and showed me one of the museum's eighteen guestbooks, which included notes from Stalin's daughter and from tourists who had come from every Soviet republic. When I came to the garden museum a second time, Ushangi Davidovich wasn't home—he was at a meeting of a new communist party called "Russia is Our Friend."

I ask my neighbors, who are afraid of getting fired: "Do you like your life under capitalism?"

Very often with older Georgians, asking questions in Russian led to discussions of Georgian–Russian relations. There are a lot of retiree taxi drivers in Tbilisi, and after I got in almost every one of them would start a conversation along the following lines:

> "70 percent of Georgians believe that we would be better off living in Russia than in Europe or America. We get grants from the West, but everything goes to the elites, not the people. There's nothing to do in Tbilisi because of unemployment—almost all the manufacturers are at a standstill. In Soviet times, we had work and there was more consideration for the people. Our pensions are 160 lari—can you imagine living on that?"

The taxi drivers ignored me when I brought up Russia's economic crisis and the political repression happening there. "If only we had a president like Putin!" I heard over and over again.

a refugee from Sukhumi

—Blame the war on the people who said that Georgia is only for Georgians.

An old man, a refugee from Sukhumi, began a conversation with me on the bus. "I wasn't a communist in Soviet times," he said. "I was critical of the regime. Looking back, I see that things were better back then. Free education and healthcare for all. My son fought, he was injured, and the government didn't provide for his treatment. I feel very hurt by our state."

ARMENIANS IN TBILISI

Georgians and Armenians are neighbors whose history and culture are inextricably linked, but they're very different to be around. When I was in Yerevan, I noticed that Armenians tended to be analytical, quick to clock logical fallacies or factual inconsistencies. In Tbilisi, the most important thing is to amuse and be amused, to be lively and creative. My new friend Lus, who is Armenian, recently moved from Yerevan to Tbilisi. She agreed with my assessment.

— If I let myself relax, I'll become an outcast. You're not allowed to act sad here.

I showed my drawing of Lus to my Georgian friends. Here's what they said:

"It's true, you're not allowed to be sad in Georgia. The only kind of negative behavior that's more or less socially acceptable is aggression. We've never learned to cope with sadness. If you delve too deep into your emotions, you might find even more terrifying stuff in there."

"Demonstrative happiness improves your social standing. Everything's going well in your life—you're not whining or weeping."

"Georgians don't like weakness. It's part of our culture."

Armenians are the second largest minority in Georgia after Azerbaijanis (5 percent versus 6 percent).

— Until the '90s, Tbilisi was like an ajapsandali, a vegetable dish with everything mixed up together. Nobody knew anyone else's nationality.

The ancestors of many local Armenians came to Georgia as refugees fleeing the genocide. Yana was born in Tbilisi, and her great-grandfather and great-grandmother were Armenians who moved here at that time. She grew up speaking Russian at home and learned Armenian and Georgian in college.

People are not especially warm toward Armenians in Georgia today. The Georgians I asked about this told me things like:

> "There were more Armenians than Georgians here before the revolution. They ran trade and Georgians would come from the villages and work for them, like migrant workers."

> "Georgians don't live in Armenia, but a lot of Armenians live in Georgia. They own property and businesses here. A large Armenian diaspora is a potential threat."

Almost all the artists and activists I met in Yerevan travel to Georgia multiple times a year. There are many more Western organizations in Georgia, and thus more opportunities. Many of my younger friends from Tbilisi have never been to Armenia. When I'd ask them about how they felt about the ElectroYerevan protests of 2015 or other demonstrations, they'd tell me that they read more about what was happening in Turkey, or that they usually followed the protests in Greece.

In Tbilisi, I took part in a project called Working Agenda of Amiran/Mher. One of its goals was to strengthen the cultural ties between Georgia and Armenia. The Georgian participants talked about how they couldn't break away from Europe: "We need to value the European Experience. We have a Global Future."

"In every conversation we have, it feels like Armenians are supposed to acknowledge how right and good it is to follow the European path and how bad everything is under the Russian yoke," said Zara, an activist from Armenia, after the discussion. Young, progressive Armenians have a negative view of Russian influence in Armenia, but they also do not idealize Georgia's dependence on the West.

AZERBAIJANIS IN TBILISI

The Armenians invited their Azerbaijani friends to the project's closing dinner. Many Armenians in Tbilisi told me that, despite all their conflicts, Armenians and Azerbaijanis understand one another better than Georgians do. From the Azerbaijanis I heard that no one was as close to them as the Armenians.

I met Azerbaijani writer Seymur Baycan, who gave me a copy of his book *Gugark*, about the Karabakh war. In *Gugark,* Seymur recalls the first shots exchanged between Armenians and Azerbaijanis in his hometown of Fuzuli, the beginning of the combat that leveled the city to ruins; and his family's move to Baku. I found the book's descriptions of domestic violence harder to read than its war stories: beatings of women and children were written about as mundane daily occurrences.

Seymur entered the Baku cultural scene in the 2000s. Then, beginning in 2009, the government started forcing the active, artistic intelligentsia out of the country. I later met Seymur's friends, a couple that had been forced to leave Baku due to government pressure. They were the journalist, translator, and poet Gunel Movlud and her husband, Haci Haciyev, a doctor.

Gunel started out as a blogger. After a series of critical texts about the problems in Azerbaijani society, she became one of the country's most read authors. Today, Gunel is an editor for Meydan TV, a media organization founded by Azerbaijani dissidents in Berlin.

Most of Gunel's reporting is about women's rights in the Southern Caucasus. "The lives of Azerbaijani and Georgian women in Tbilisi are very different," she said. "Azerbaijani families take girls out of school when they're in the ninth grade. They marry them off when they're 14. If the girls resist, that's basically suicide. Our son's nanny became a grandmother at 32. Talk to her."

Renka, Gunel's nanny, agreed to pose for a portrait and told me a little bit about herself. She was 13 when she got married and gave birth to her daughter when she was 14. At 19, she had her second child, a son. For a long time, Renka worked around the house with her kids and only went out in the city with her husband. She started nannying recently, and she really likes it. Here's what she had to say about unmarried, independent women: "They have money and do what they want. That seems better to me."

There's a Caucasian term for correct social behavior: "namus," in Azerbaijani and Armenian, and "namusi" in Georgian. For men, "namus" means honor and conscience. For women, namus has to do with sexual behavior and its unacceptability. In the Northern Caucausus it is said that a man with an unfaithful female relative can only cleanse his namus by killing her.

Seymur said that in Azerbaijani society, namus can be bought. If a woman is a well-paid actress or singer, she can come home late with a new man every night if she wants to.

RUSSIANS IN TBILISI

My friends told me that a lot of young people from Russia who are opposed to Putin's regime have started moving to Tbilisi over the past few years. There aren't that many of them yet. The ones I met chose Georgia because, as one of them said, "you don't need a visa; it's warm, cheap, and close; a lot of people speak Russian; and there are a lot of cultural similarities." They're not sure that they will be able to settle in Georgia in the long term, but they are not prepared to move back to Russia. Yan, a former Moscow activist, is one of these semi-migrants. "All of Georgia is like one big village: the values are more patriarchal and people are a lot closer to one another than they are in Russia. There's less aggression, but Georgians' irresponsibility gets on my nerves," he said.

> in my opinion the diferrence bethwen georgian and european people is that we mostly thow garbage in nature. in georgea women can't do what they really want, becouse public

Yan

Nodar

Yan rents an apartment with his girlfriend Ani, whom he met in Tbilisi, and her brother Nodar. Like many other young Georgians, Nodar doesn't speak Russian, and we couldn't quite get a conversation going in our bad English. I asked Nodar to write what he thought was special about Georgian society on this drawing.

Yan reads the news from Russia less and less frequently, and when he does, it makes him grateful about having managed to flee the "total insanity."

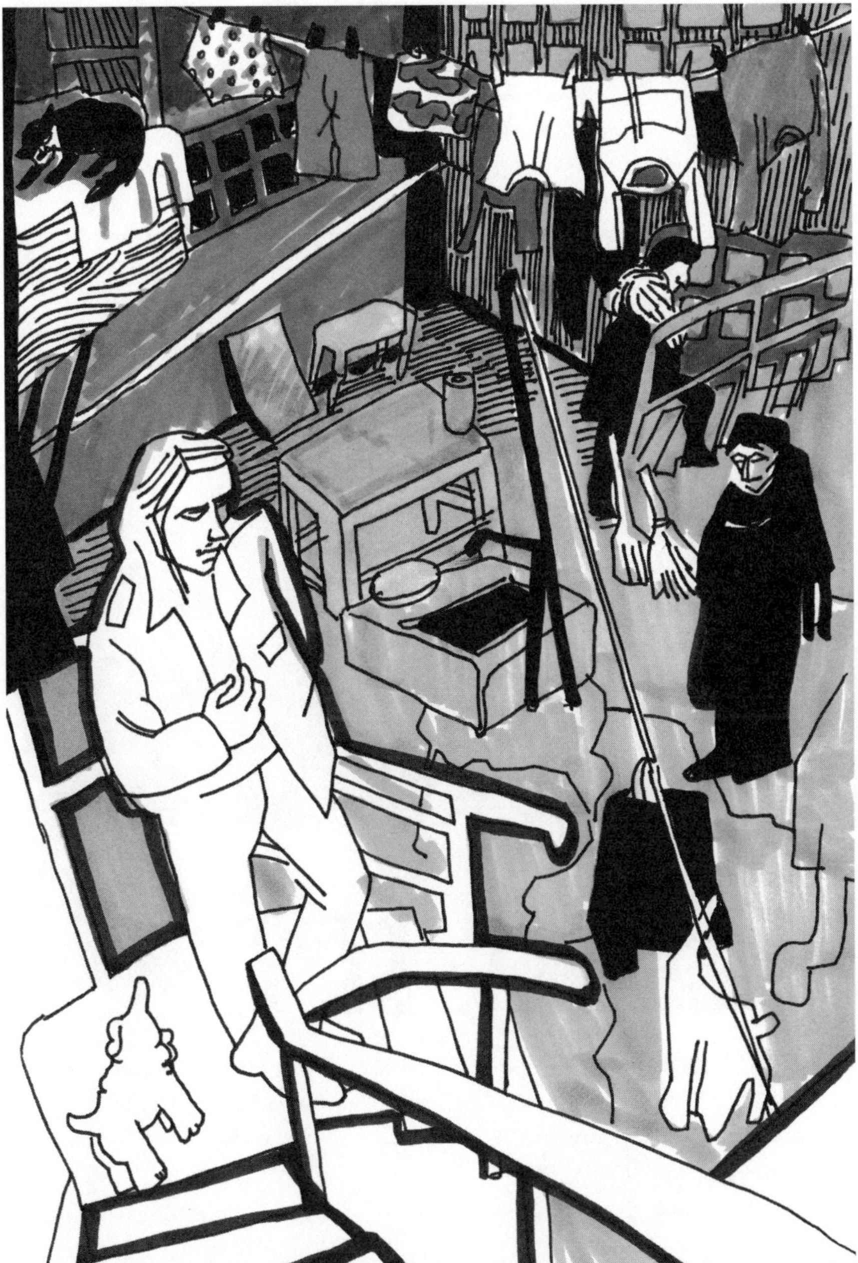

You can always find Russians at the Kiwi Cafe in downtown Tbilisi. When it opened in 2015, it was the first vegan cafe in Georgia. Its founders are an international crew from Georgia, Russia, Iran, and Sweden. Their initial concept was making extremely simple, extremely cheap food, but little by little, the cafe has turned into a trendy tourist spot. Activists from Russia living in Georgia for an indeterminate period can be found working in the kitchen.

Kiwi Cafe regularly hosts screenings, discussions, and lectures on social and political subjects. I went to a lecture on Kurdish resistance delivered by Alexey, an activist from Yekaterinburg.

Alexey moved to Tbilisi with a group of friends. "We've been living here for two months. I haven't run into any police or any bureaucrats. In Russia, it feels like they're everywhere, and you're the one who doesn't belong."

Oleg is a former journalist from Moscow and one of the founders of Kiwi Cafe.

He told me about his two most recent trips back to Russia. The first time, Oleg crossed the border on land through the checkpoint in the village of Verkhnii Lars. "The FSB searched me and my bags. They suspected me of being in ISIS." The second time, he flew to Moscow with a Ukrainian friend. The Ukrainian passport, residency permit in Zakarpattia, and tattoos were enough to get his friend detained and deported. "You're not even officially in Russia yet, and it's already clear what you're going back to!" Oleg said.

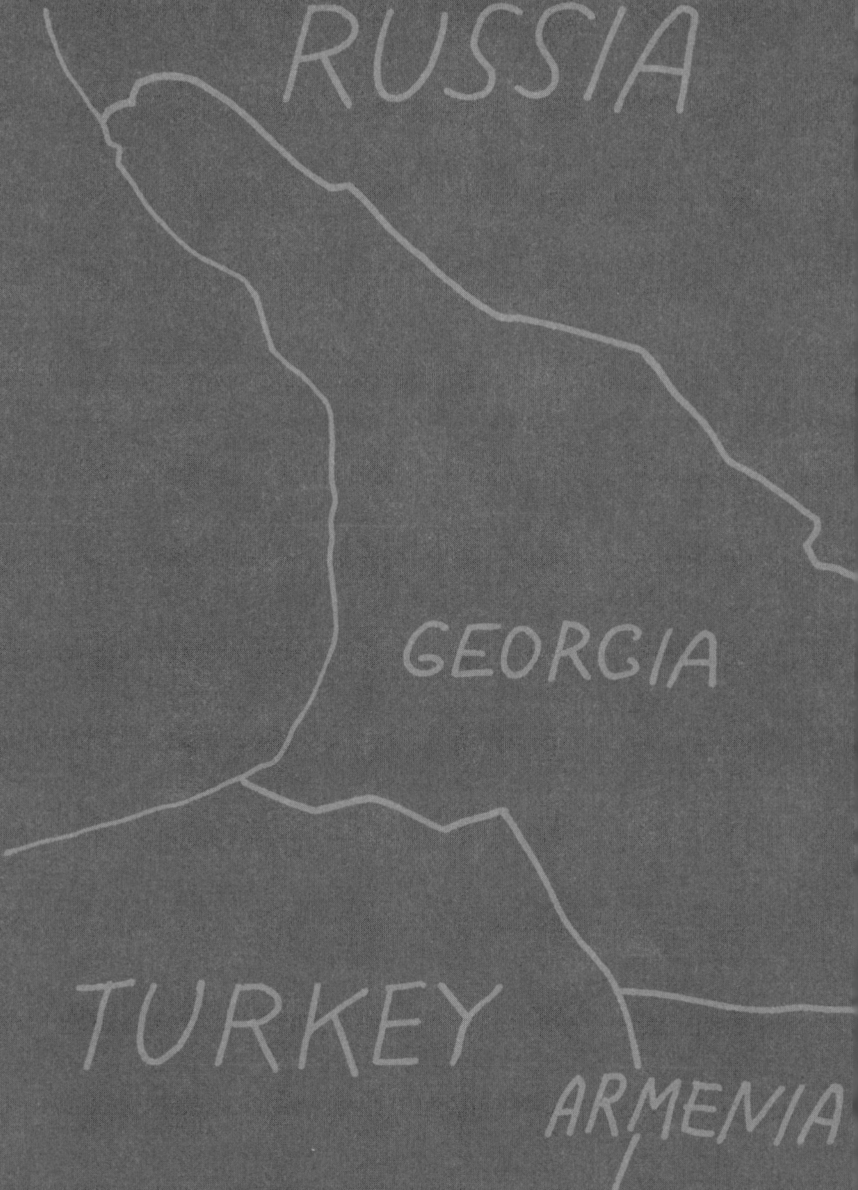
RUSSIA
GEORGIA
TURKEY
ARMENIA

A TRIP TO INGUSHETIA, 2017

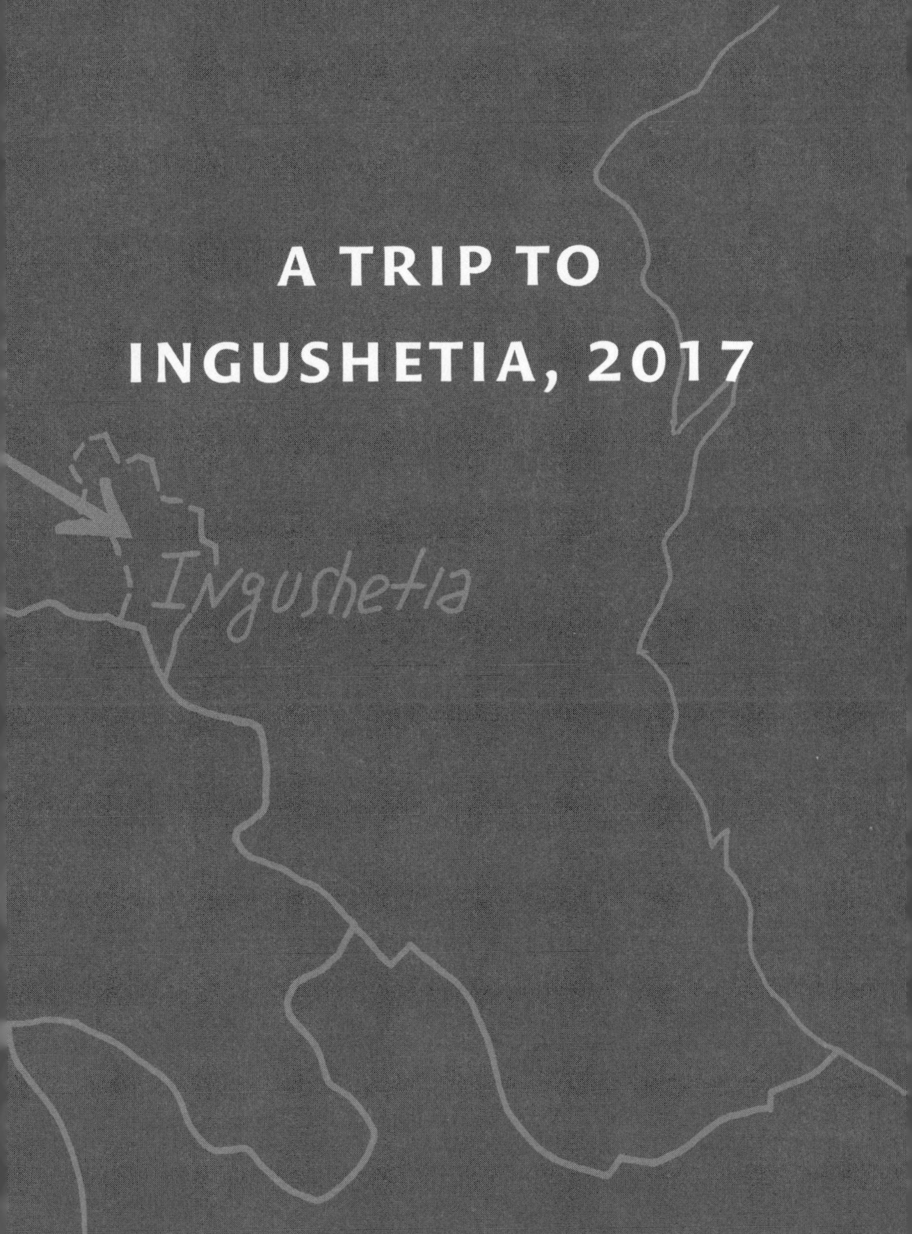
Ingushetia

INSTEAD OF AMAZONS

There are places where the question of who has come to do the reporting is a critical one: a male journalist or a female journalist, a male artist or a female artist. In some places, I can be an invisible observer watching the protagonists of my stories; in others, I become the observed. In Ingushetia, where I went to lead master classes for women's groups and draw a new chapter for this book, I became the center of attention.

Even at the airport, I noticed that besides me and an obviously non-local blonde, there were no other women in jeans. As it turned out, Ingushetian men believe that it's inappropriate for Ingushetian women to wear pants. If one were to dare to go outside dressed that way, she could receive a lecture from any passing man and cars might stop and honk. With my semi-shaved head, which unequivocally marked me as a foreigner, I was able to go around wearing jeans unmolested. It was only children who were shocked upon encountering such a strange creature—a lady couldn't wear pants and have a haircut like that, and a man couldn't have earrings. Pointing their fingers at me, they'd anxiously ask their parents, "Why is that boy wearing earrings?"

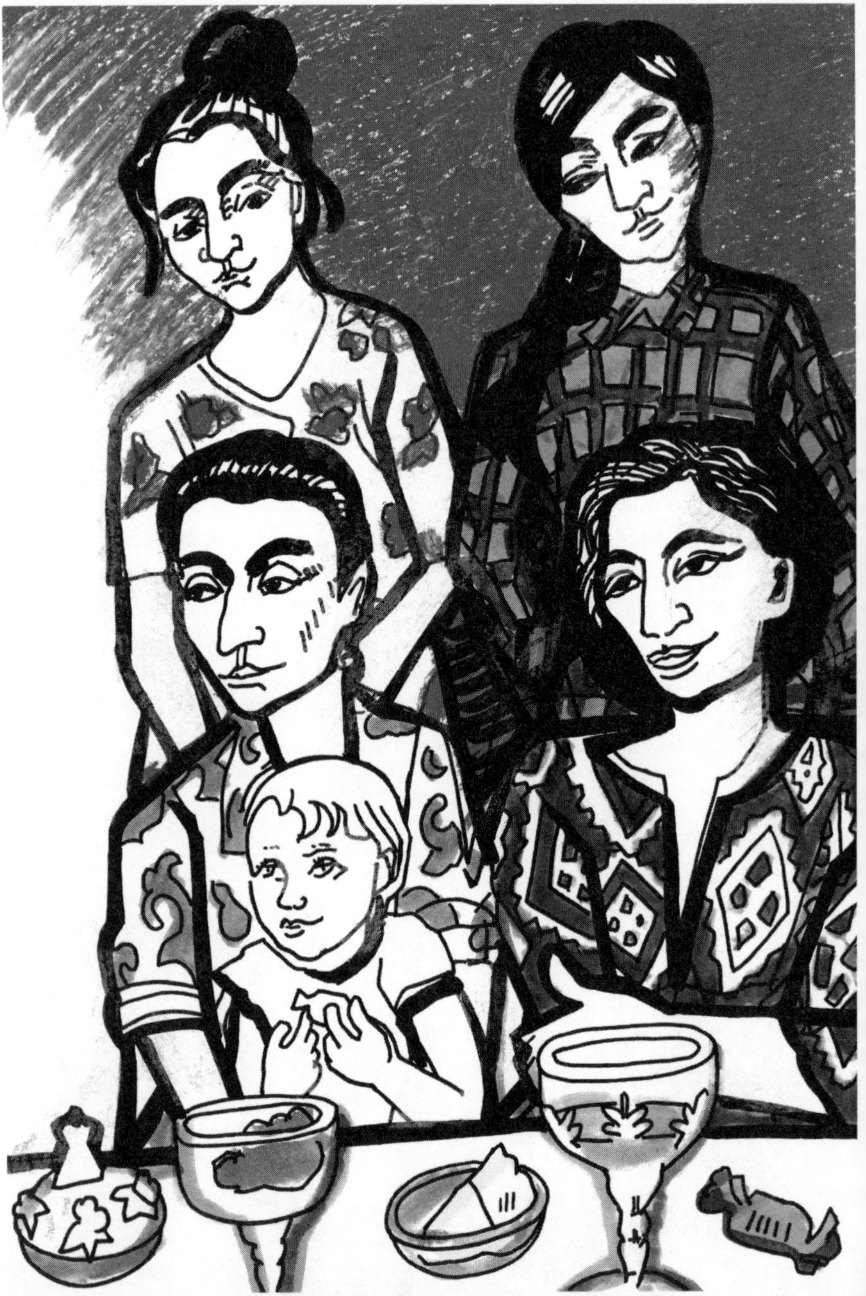

The male control of women's appearance turned out to be a hot topic in my workshops about socially engaged graphic art. One of the participants drew what she called "the council of Aksakalovs"—her grandfather, father, and younger brother talking about whether she was allowed to paint her nails. The responses? "Not black." "Not red." "No."

Another important topic was marriage: what would it mean to enter a husband's family where a woman would be expected to serve the entire clan?

—Like every girl my age, I'm scared of getting married. You have to figure out what kind of home you're walking into, so you don't find yourself in a trap.

According to local lore, this was once the home of the Amazons. If you imagine their absolute opposite, that is the paragon a modern day Ingushetian woman should aspire to. Ideally, she should look like the only statue of a woman in Magas, a young mother of three with a dress down to the ground. Really, every member of Ingushetian society is required to play their role. In Ingushetian culture, there's even a concept known as *Ezdel*—a set of unwritten rules that, if violated, will transform you into a pariah.

This is what one of my master class students said about my life in Moscow. I understand where she's coming from—that's the happiness that pushed me to escape the provinces. Of course, in Serpukhov, the Russian town where I was born, women's lives aren't controlled like they are in Ingushetia. But my determination to become an artist made people laugh at me. It made them feel uncomfortable. Compared to that, the indifference I encountered in Moscow was more appealing. Many years later, after I started working in the West, I saw that in addition to societies that are hostile toward people and societies that simply don't care, there is a third way: societies where individuality is valued. And, indeed, where that individuality sells.

VICTIMS OF REPRESSIONS

During my trip to Dagestan, I learned a lot about the 1944 deportation of Chechens. Their stories were told by the Dagestanis who'd been forced live in the homes the Chechens left behind. Now I heard the stories of the Ingushetians. During World War II, they were deported to Central Asia alongside the Chechens. Officially, these nations were accused of being Nazi collaborators; the real reasons for their deportations remain unknown. Almost every elderly person I spoke to in Ingushetia had been born in Kazakhstan.

These events were commemorated by the Memorial Complex of Memory and Glory, located between Magas, the capital, and Narzan, the republic's largest city. I led one of my master classes there. A girl who participated in the class told me that in her family, the grandmothers and grandfathers on both sides met on the trains returning from exile.

While I was waiting for the master class to start, I counted 57 family members among the deported.
Jamila

The first thing that visitors to the Memorial see is a large bas-relief that depicts Ingushetians swearing fealty to the Russian empire in 1770. In the middle of the courtyard, there is a monument to the Ingushetians who served in the so-called Savage Division of the Russian Imperial Army.

The Nine Towers building has a small museum. *Exile, Expulsion, The Road of Death*—these are some of the titles of the paintings in the museum. A painting called *Black Wednesday* shows a group of Soviet soldiers in hats with red stars surrounding an Ingushetian boy wearing the same kind of hat and a young mother with an infant in her arms. The other children in the room are hurriedly getting dressed to leave, and some of them are helping their grandmother put on her shoes. There are no men in the room—they're off fighting the Nazis. The walls of the deported family's home are hung with portraits of their grandfathers, who had been officers in the Russian Army.

Directly under the paintings, there are display cases with certificates and medals awarded to Ingushetians who fought with distinction in World War II. Locals say that Ingushetians were even deported from the army. The most capable soldiers had their last names changed to Russian and Ossetian ones by their commanders in order to keep them from being deported.

I asked the people I was staying with in Ingushetia what they thought about the museum.

housewife Maret

—The paintings are there so we won't forget. The medals are there so no one will mess with us.

THE OSSETIAN CONFLICT

It feels like every Ingushetian is traumatized. Some lived through deportation. Others ran from Grozny during the Chechen war. Then there are those who were forced to leave their homes behind during the East Prigorodny conflict.

— He's from Prigorodny. They had to carry him out of there on a stretcher — he was shell-shocked.

The Prigorodny District was the site of the earliest Ingushetian inhabitation. At the time of the deportations, in the 1940s, the district was annexed to the republic of North Ossetia, which it remains a part of. In 1992, an armed conflict began between the Osssetians and the Ingushetians in East Prigorodny.

On one of the evenings I was there, people insisted that I go see a woman named Patimat, whose husband and three sons disappeared during the East Prigorodny Conflict. She made every effort to track them down, writing to every authority and organizing protests in Moscow alongside other Ingushetians who'd lost their relatives. She even appeared on a TV show called *Wait For Me*. Over the past twenty-five years, she'd collected a bag full of excuses and boilerplate answers from Moscow. "Write to Vladikavkaz," she was told, the capital of North Ossetia. "We know where the mass graves are," Patimat said. "But the Ossetians won't let us excavate it to do DNA analysis."

—I used to beg God, "Don't let me find them dead!" Now I just want to find them, dead or alive.

Patimat

Patimat's neighbor Yakha told me the story of her escape from East Prigorodny with nine children via a mountain trail no more than forty centimeters wide. Volunteers from Sunzhi led the refugees down that path. Afterward, the Ingushetians took to calling it the Road of Life.

— I had to make my way down to the village, but there was no trail. All of a sudden my daughter fell into a crevasse. Luckily the ground was sandy.

Both women wanted the story of the unjust suffering of the Ingushetian people to be known outside of Ingushetia. They blessed me for drawing and writing.

FORMER STANITSAS

The town of Sunzha sits on the site of the former Cossack stanitsa, or village, of Sleptsovskaya. There were Russian Cossacks living there during the deportation of the Ingushetians. There is a dramatic contrast between the large, new, red-brick Ingushetian houses and the little Cossack houses with their closed shutters. (I was told that an Ingushetian will refuse himself everything to ensure that his home will be no worse than his neighbor's.) After the Ingushetians returned to their native land, this place became the site of ethnic conflict.

I realized that if I wanted to find some Russians, I had to go to church. The Ingushetian security guards sitting in the booth outside the churchyard searched my backpack without explanation. There were services taking place in the church, and I managed to see the entirety of the town's tiny Russian community—everyone who was able to had left these places.

When they found out that I was from Moscow, the Russians started telling me scary stories about what had happened to them here: bullying in school, kidnapped relatives, church bombings. Someone's father was killed. Because of an armed attack a few years ago, everyone coming into the church still gets searched. "Russians were settled here during the deportation," I was told. "When the Ingushetians came back, they told us, 'This is my house. You have two days to leave.' They murdered entire families."

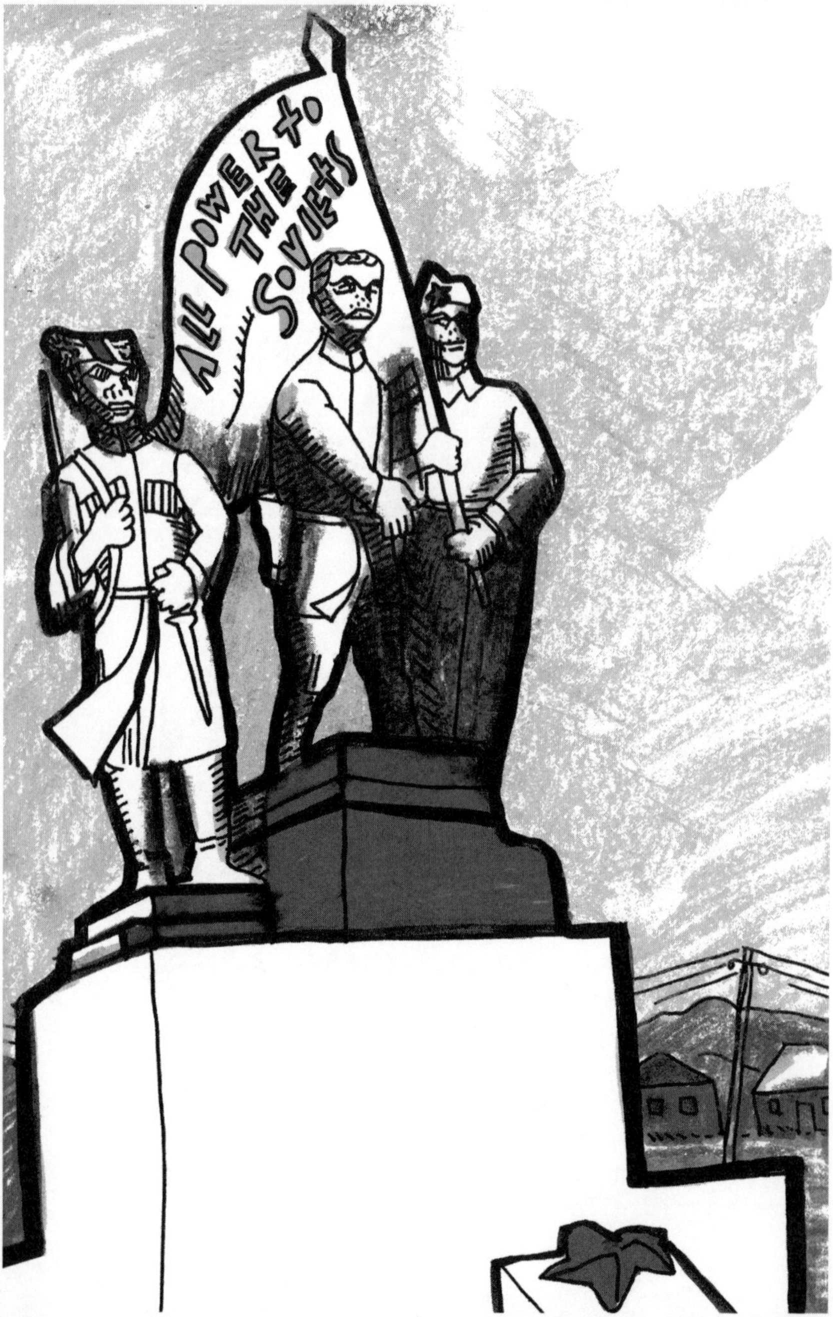
ALL POWER to THE SOVIETS

When we were saying our goodbyes, the Russians advised me to be more careful:

"Don't take off your head covering, don't wear pants," someone said. "You look like an Ingushetian. Keep your mouth shut and you'll pass."

"I tell everyone I'm from Moscow," I responded.

"No! They must think that you're gathering information for the FSB. That's what they're afraid of."

It feels like Russia is always sending Russians here, and that those Russians always turn out to be entirely unwanted once the political regime changes. The Cossacks who had participated in the colonization of the North Caucasus during the Russian Empire were de-Cossackized by the Soviets between 1918 and 1921 and deported. Then, the Cossacks that the Soviets settled here in the 1940s to take the place of the Ingushetians became extraneous after the fall of the Soviet Union. Now the Putin regime is shipping in FSB agents instead of Cossacks.

I couldn't find any Russians in the neighboring village of Troitsky. Only the monuments in the former Cossack village spoke of the Soviet past. I asked Ingushetians why they hadn't been taken down. "It wasn't the monuments that deported us, sister," they told me. Even so, the statues have gotten their noses knocked off.

INGUSH TOWERS

Established in 1994, Magas is the youngest capital city in the Russian Federation. Even the trees haven't had time to grow in yet. There is a good number of Russians living here alongside the Ingushetians, including FSB agents and their families. There was a large residential complex constructed just for them, with special schools and a daycare.

The city was celebrating the twenty-fifth anniversary of the foundation of the Ingushetian republic during my visit. I saw a stage bedecked with giant screens, and behind the stage there was an awkward-looking tower, a replica of the medieval structures. Behind the tower was a large expanse of empty plain. My trip to Ingushetia depressed me. It felt like I was moving around among hurriedly assembled set decorations in a space that had been scorched of all of its history.

There were some important-looking men declaiming on the stage: "Because of Putin's heroic efforts, today, Russia—and, by extension, Ingushetia—is developing successfully. All hail the friendship of the nations and the unity of Russia!" If you spoke to regular Ingushetians, you would hear totally different things. "People come after you Russians for your political views. They come after us a priori because of our nationality."

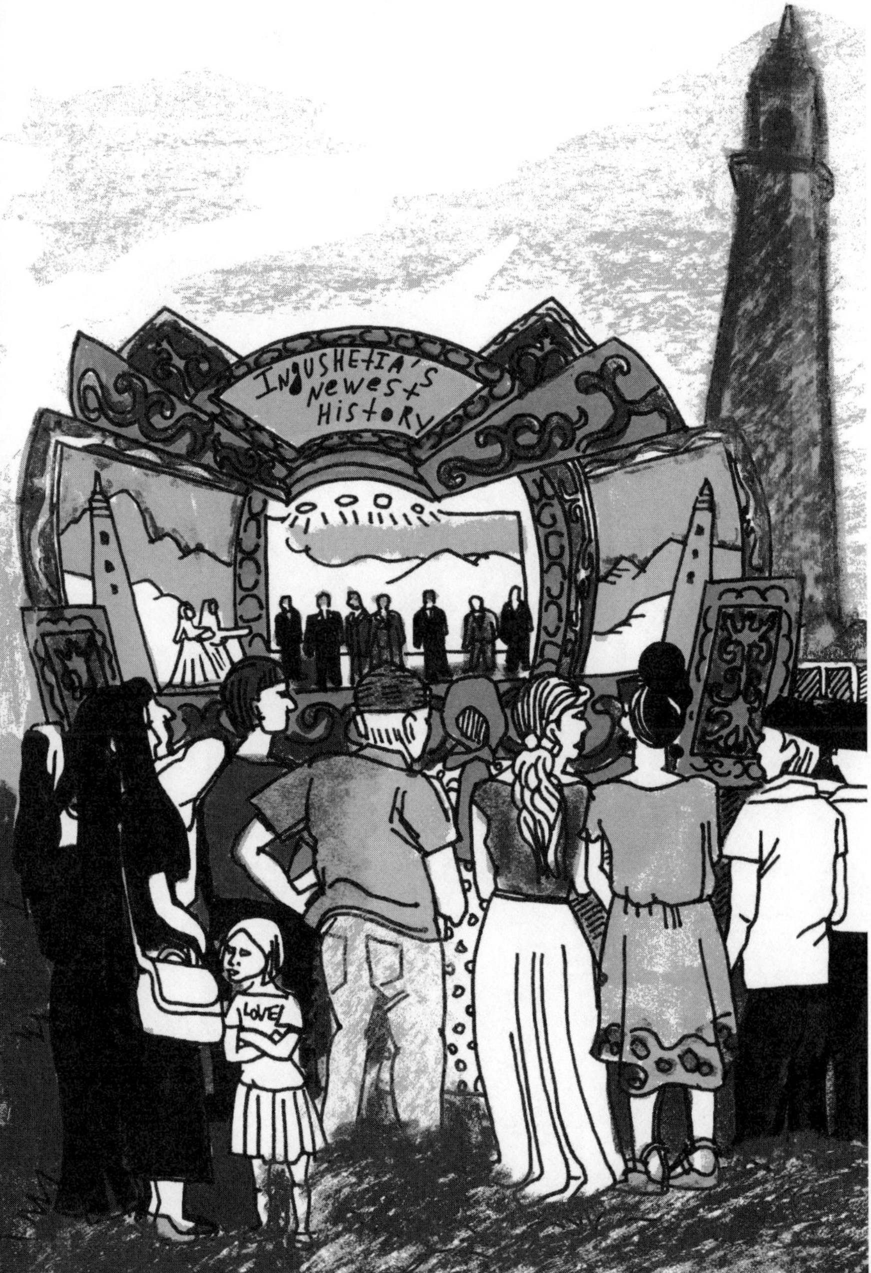
Ingushetia's Newest History
LOVE!

When I shared my impressions with the Ingushetian family I was staying with, they offered to take me out to the mountains to show me the Ingush towers. I knew that the Ingushetians had once been a mountain people, but I didn't know that the local mountains were full of medieval settlements.

We first passed through Magas with its boring new construction and then through the villages with their red brick houses. Then the hills began, and finally, the mountains. The towers stood on the mountain slopes like pikes stuck into the ground, tips up. Every family was supposed to build their own tower.

We got out of the car and climbed up into the mountains. For this ascent even the daughter of the family had put on pants—she couldn't be expected to trek up a slope overgrown with wild grasses while wearing a skirt. A friend of the father, a documentary filmmaker, told us about the structures we were taking pictures of: medieval homes and defensive towers, sunny ancient burial grounds and pagan shrines. On the facade of one of the shrines we even found the remains of a bas-relief illustrated with mythical characters.

The director pointed out the holes in the walls of some of the towers and said that these were bullet holes. During the deportation of the Ingushetians, their towers were partially destroyed by Soviet soldiers. "Russia can destroy," said the father of the family, "but it can never restore."

We came to the banks of a mountain river, and the men made us shish kebabs. This small group of people was gathering strength among their ancient settlements. Time stopped.

KAZAKHSTAN

UZBEKISTAN

TURKMEMSTAN

TRAVELS TO OSH, 2016–17

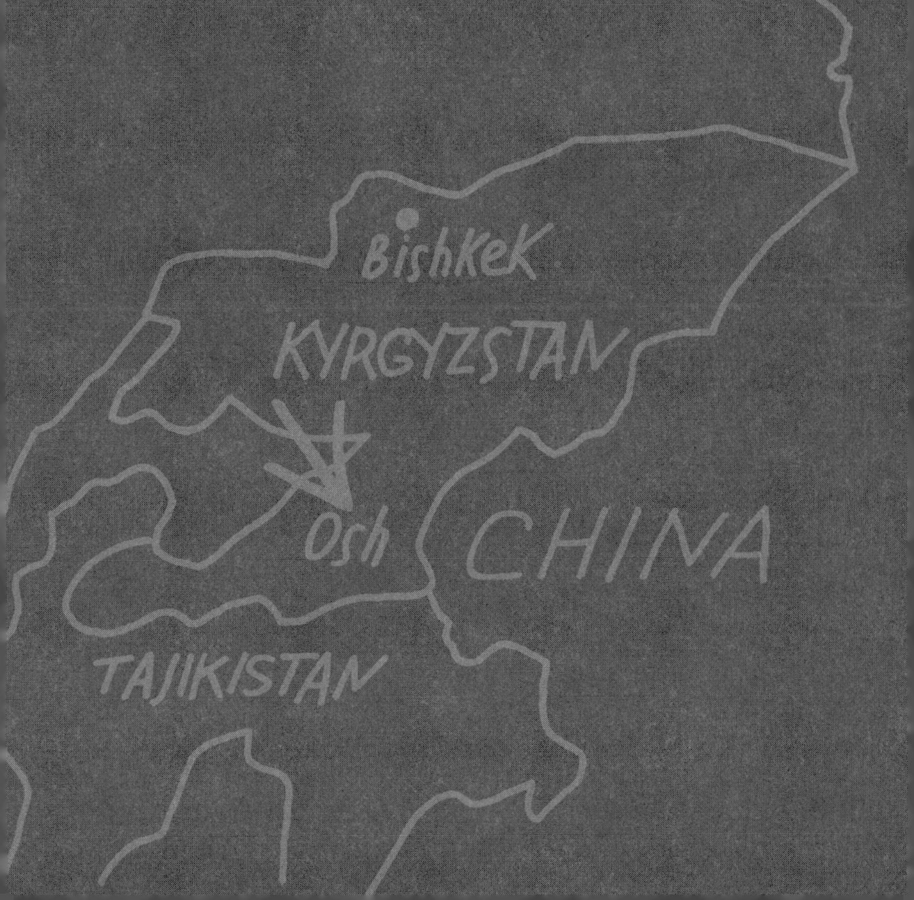
Bishkek
KYRGYZSTAN
Osh
CHINA
TAJIKISTAN

A SMALL TOWN

"That's funny! What are you, a famous artist, doing in that small, apolitical town no one cares about?" asked a friend from Bishkek when I told him that I was spending a month in Osh. Osh is, in fact, the second most important city in Kyrgyzstan after Bishkek, the capital. But it really is small.

If anyone outside of Kyrgyzstan has heard of Osh, it's likely because of the bloody 2010 conflict between Kyrgyzstanis and Uzbeks. Osh is on the border with Uzbekistan, and a lot of ethnic Uzbeks live in the area. Everyone from Osh with whom I discussed these events recalled horrific details, but today, the city appears quiet, its residents calm and relaxed. Both the conflict and the resolution are commemorated in the central square with a statue of two mothers, Kyrgyz and Uzbek, embracing over a bassinet with the names of the deceased.

The Kyrgyz people I talked to described their society as enlightened and open to outside influence. Uzbeks, on the other hand, were proud of having a society that's traditional, hermetic, and religious. "I think that the only reason Osh survived was because of the Uzbeks," my Kyrgyz friend told me. "They get up at 5, sweep the streets, go to work at the market. Kyrgyz people wake up at 9 and go to the office, where they spend their days doing corruption."

AT NEW RHYTHM

I came to Osh to lead master classes in feminist stencil art at the youth organization New Rhythm. The workshops were attended by very young women, only one of whom was Uzbek. Her name was Madina. Madina made a stencil about early marriages in Uzbek families and talked about how her parents were pressuring her to get married. "Only my grandmothers want me to stay in school," Madina said. "And they're happy when I wear short dresses." Other workshop participants seconded this story—their Soviet grandmothers, they said, were the most progressive people in their families, advising their granddaughters to study languages and travel the world.

Uzbek and Kyrgyz children play together on the playground. But none of my Kyrgyz master class students had Uzbek girlfriends. Their lives are too different: from the age of 12 or 13, as soon as they get their periods, many Uzbek girls are made to stay home. If you see girls in Osh with short haircuts and wearing shorts, you can be sure that they're Kyrgyz. Women and girls in long robes and hijabs will most likely be Uzbek.

There were other volunteers teaching at New Rhythm. The majority of Kyrgyz NGOs working in education, culture, and human rights exist due to the support of grants from the West. New Rhythm's organizers counted no fewer than fifteen human rights organizations in Osh. In 2014, there was a bill under discussion in Kyrgyzstan that copied Russia's 2012 so-called foreign-agent law, according to which NGOs that receive financial support from abroad are required to register as foreign agents. In Russia, organizations that find themselves on that list are constantly audited and fined, it becomes too difficult for foreign donors to work with them, and regular citizens who don't usually concern themselves with politics believe that these foreign agents are really dangerous spies. The law didn't pass in Kyrgyzstan.

I attended lectures conducted by European volunteers who talked about activism and sex education and HIV in Kyrgyzstan. The lectures were in English. Progressive Kyrgyz youth are actively learning the language.

Russia doesn't put any money toward the development of civic society in Kyrgyzstan. My visit was paid for by a European foundation.

TRACES OF EMPIRE

Osh is one of the most ancient cities in Central Asia—it was part of the Khanate of Kokand. In 1876, after many years of colonial wars, the Khanate was incorporated into the Russian Empire. The Alay Kyrgyz people continued resisting the so-called "white Tsar" for some time afterwards, under the leadership of their ruler Kurmanjan Datka. But they were outmatched, and she was eventually forced to assent to the annexation of the Alay District. There is a monument to this legendary ruler on Osh's main street.

The Russian army was accompanied by artist Vasily Vereshchagin, perhaps the first Russian orientalist artist. Vereshchagin drew military battles, local architecture, and scenes from the lives of the fighters. Then, when locals revolted, the artist would pick up a rifle and participate in putting down the revolts. "I remember I shot two of the people attacking us methodically, if I can put it that way, like a professor," he wrote in his book *At War in Asia and Europe*. I admire Vereshchagin's courage and talent, but I am repulsed by his involvement in this war. I went to the National Historical and Archaeological Museum Complex Sulayman in Osh in search of something related to the artist's work, but found nothing.

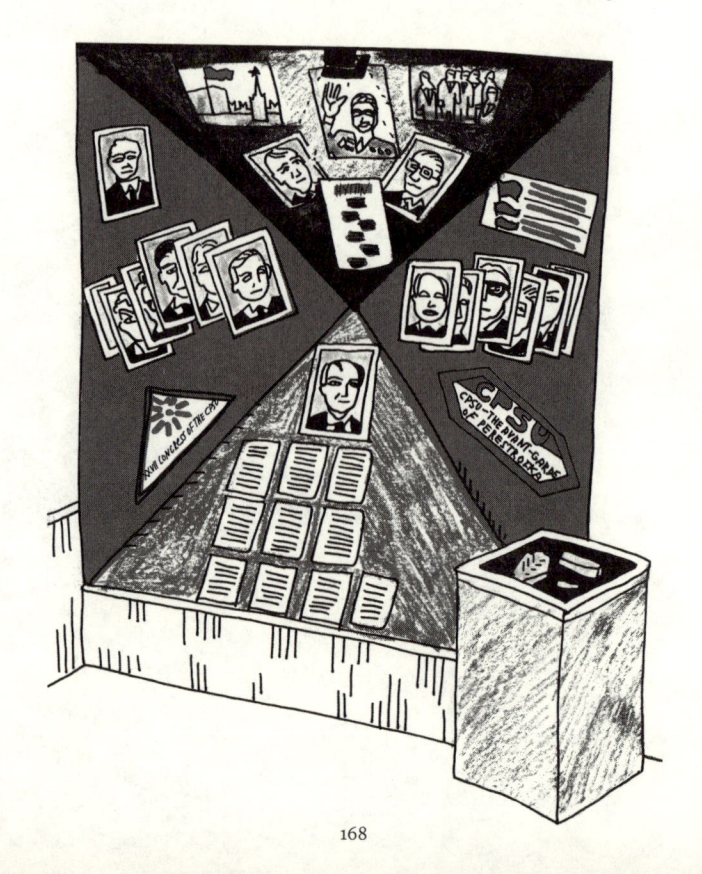

"All of the trade routes would bypass us because we had nothing to offer," a guide told me as she led me through the collection. "After the Russians came, we got samovars and porcelain. We found out about irons. We got Singer sewing machines. We learned the calendar—my great-grandmothers and grandfathers didn't know their own birthdays. We learned about medicine, that you didn't have to die from the flu. My great-grandmother had thirteen children, but only three of them survived. After the Russians came, we finally created our own independent state."

Alongside taxidermied animals, archaeological finds, and everyday objects, I encountered a real Red Corner in the late-'70s style. Next to Lenin's call to the communists of Turkestan, there were photographs of the "active participants of collectivization": police chiefs, organizers of Komsomol and Party groups, secretaries of Komsomol committees. On another wall, there was a list of people repressed during Stalin's regime. The museum's collection ended with a photograph of Mikhail Gorbachev.

In 1991, when the Soviet Union collapsed, the Kyrgyz Soviet Republic became the independent state of Kyrgyzstan. Unlike many other former Soviet republics, they didn't get rid of any of their Soviet symbols or monuments.

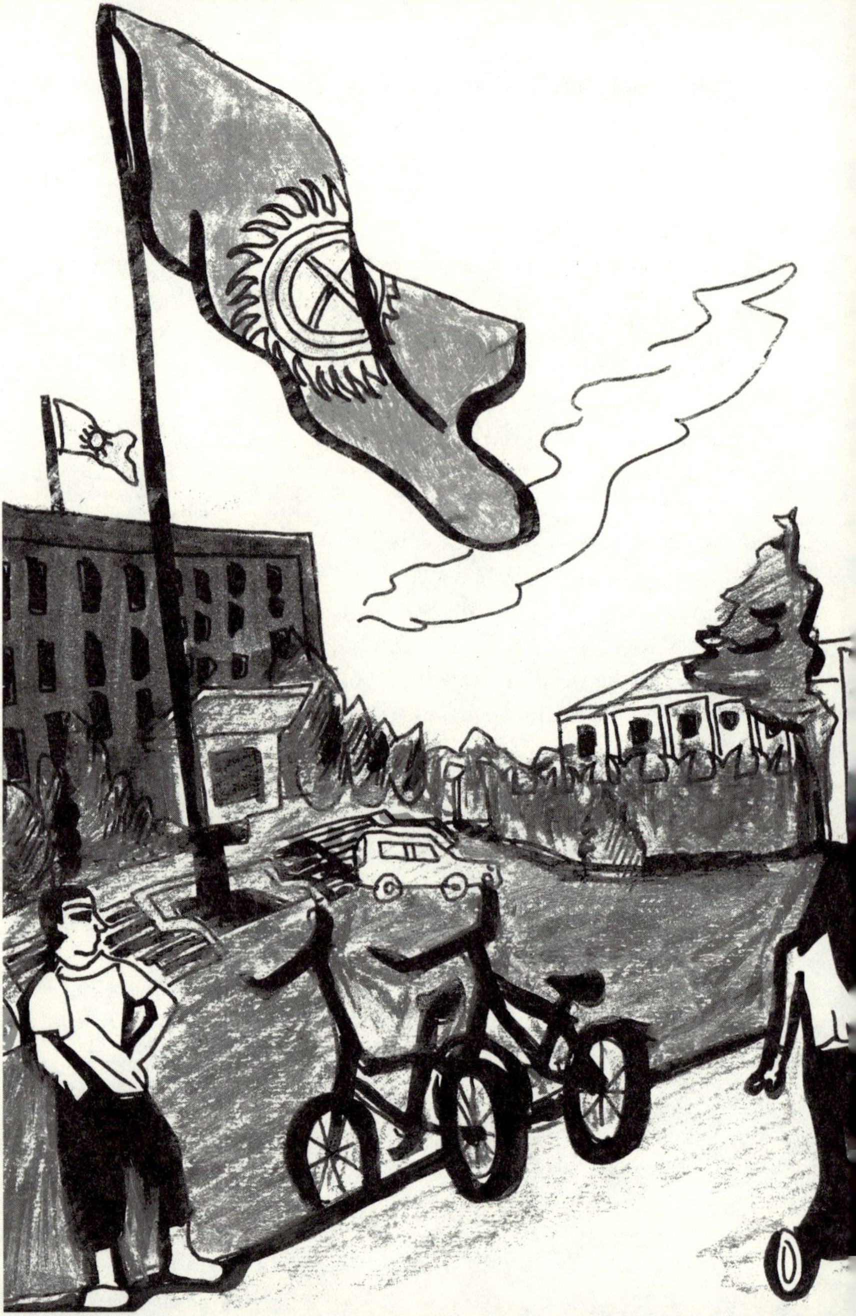

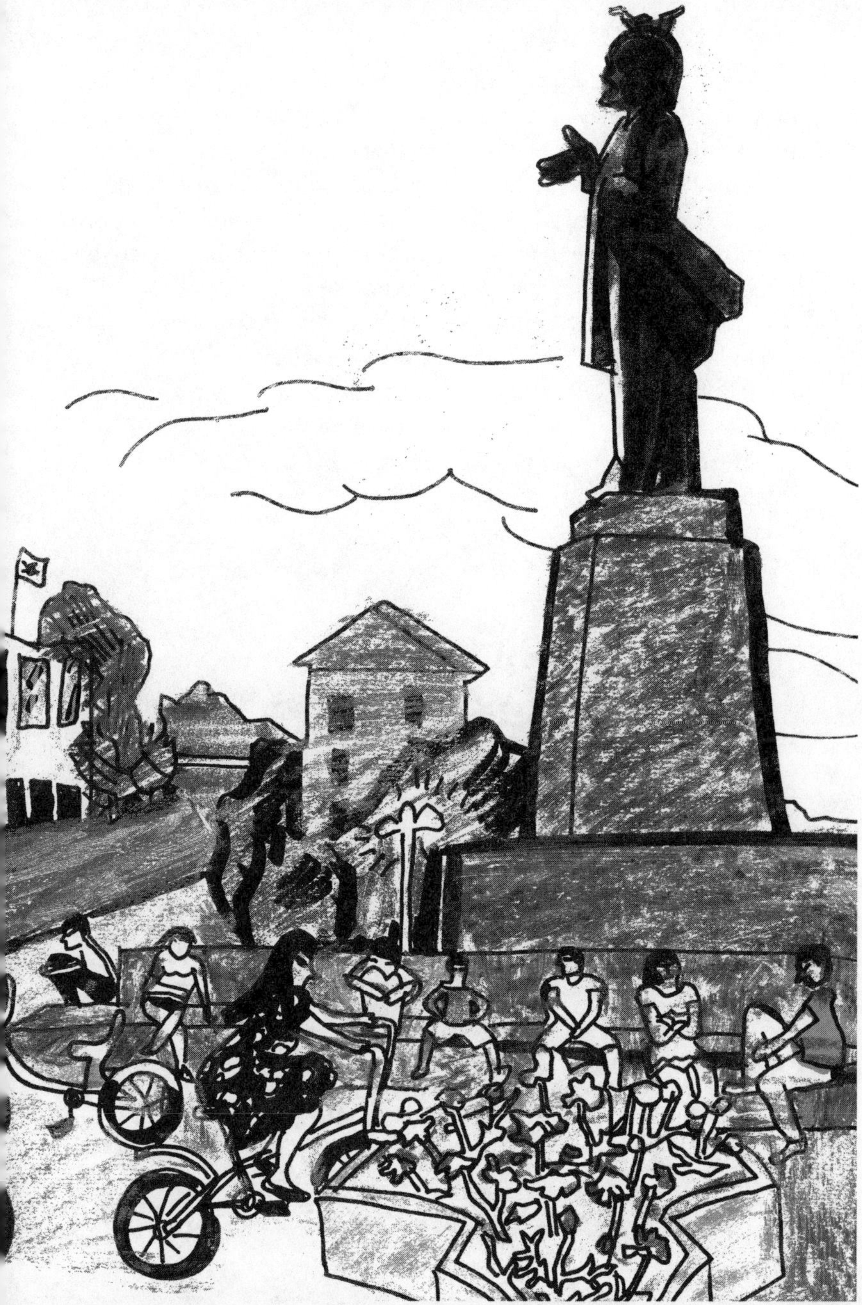

There is a big statue of Lenin on Osh's central square, in front of the city hall. They never took it down. At night, Lenin melts into the darkness; the lights are set up so that only the town hall and its giant national flag are illuminated, and not Lenin. People offered different explanations of why Lenin was left standing. "Because Lenin is our father. He gave us an education," one man told me. "It's not a tree—you can't just cut it down. It cost a lot of money," others said. Kyrgyzstan isn't a rich country—they don't have extra money lying around to systematically destroy Soviet symbolism like they had in the Baltic States, Georgia, and Ukraine. In any case, the majority of Kyrgyz people do feel loyal to their Soviet heritage.

The children playing in the square didn't know that this was a monument to Lenin. "Lenin—he's some kind of Russian hero," they said.

There's a Communist Party office in Osh, located on Lenin Street. The elderly local communists there were very happy to talk to me. "The majority of the people in Kyrgyzstan voted to preserve the Soviet Union," they told me. "The Russians believed in Lenin like he was God. We only took on the very best parts of the Communist Party and we're not about to forget that."

MIGRATION

In Soviet times, architects, builders, engineers, agronomists, teachers, doctors, and artists would move to Central Asia. Some were forcibly resettled there to work, others came of their own volition or out of ideological convictions. After the fall of the USSR, the Russians began to return to Russia, and only a few Russian families remain in Osh today. I visited one of them—the husband is a geologist who refuses to leave and the wife is a former teacher who dreams about nothing else. Their children moved away long ago.

None of the Russians I talked to complained of persecution on the basis of their nationality. Although they have lived in Kyrgyzstan for most of their lives, they don't speak a work of Kyrgyz, but don't see that as a problem, since Russian is the country's second official language, as per the Constitution. The main reason they leave is the unemployment.

> —My friend Vanya is a CEO in Kostroma. Before he came to visit me, he was convinced that everyone here went around on horseback and camels.

Hasan

    In almost every family in Osh, there's someone who has gone off to Russia for work. In Moscow, the majority of migrant workers cleaning the streets, driving the taxis, and building the buildings are Kyrgyz or Uzbek. Most often, Muscovites are condescending toward them. Even in those rare instances when they make contact, Muscovites are unlikely to be interested in Central Asian culture and prefer to imagine Kyrgyzstan as some wild, untamed place.

One of my new acquaintances in Osh told me that for a long time, he worked at a Magnolia chain grocery store in Moscow. "When I was heading home, one of my coworkers said, 'Why don't you bring back some Coca-Cola so that your people can try it?' I'd told him about Kyrgyzstan, but apparently, that whole time he kept wondering things like, 'So do you really have paved roads there?' And: 'Do you have laws there, or do you just start shooting one another anytime there's a problem?'"

> I have an easier time finding a common language with nationalists. At least they don't hide their real feelings about migrants.

In Russia, it's not just condescension that's common toward people who look Asian—they're frequently attacked. Another Osh friend, an Uzbek named Anvar, told me about how he once witnessed this kind of attack on the Moscow metro: "It was a station that had policemen on duty. Skinheads got onto a train car that had a lot of non-Russians on it. They started a brawl, but the police did nothing."

"We're part of the Russian world," Anvar told me. "I think in Russian. When I talk to my friends, we say 'Crimea is ours! And Donbass will be, too!' Just like the French, you need to accept the results of your colonialist activities."

The locals I met around town treated me with great generosity. For example, when the owner of a teahouse found out that I was a Russian from Moscow, he ordered me a celebratory plov and desserts on the house. While I was drawing Bakhtyar, he sung Russia's praises, which made me feel like some kind of orientalist artist.

ON SULAYMAN MOUNTAIN

I came to Osh twice and stayed for a month each time. In all that time, nothing of consequence happened in the city. I would just walk down the streets with signs that started out in Russian, continued in Kyrgyz, and ended in English; hang out with the young feminists from New Rhythm; and draw the women in hijabs sitting under Pepsi-branded umbrellas at the bazaars. People started saying hello to me: "We saw you drawing at the park. Where are you from? Come over sometime!"

On my last day, the feminists from New Rhythm decided to take me up to the sacred Sulayman Mountain (the Throne of King Sulayman), which rises up from the city center. According to local legend, Zarathustra developed his teachings in a cave on that mountain.

During the day, it's impossible to ascend the scorching-hot mountain slope. We came in the early morning. There were pilgrims already gathered at the foothill. I started drawing them when a young woman approached me and said that she wanted to get in my picture. I thought to myself that she had to be Uzbek, from a religious family. Suddenly, the wind lifted up the edge of her dress, and I saw that she was wearing extremely tall platform sneakers covered in pink sequins. A guy was hanging around in the background, clearly waiting for her. "We've been out here all night," she told me. "Is that your husband?" I asked. "No, just my boyfriend," she answered, laughing.

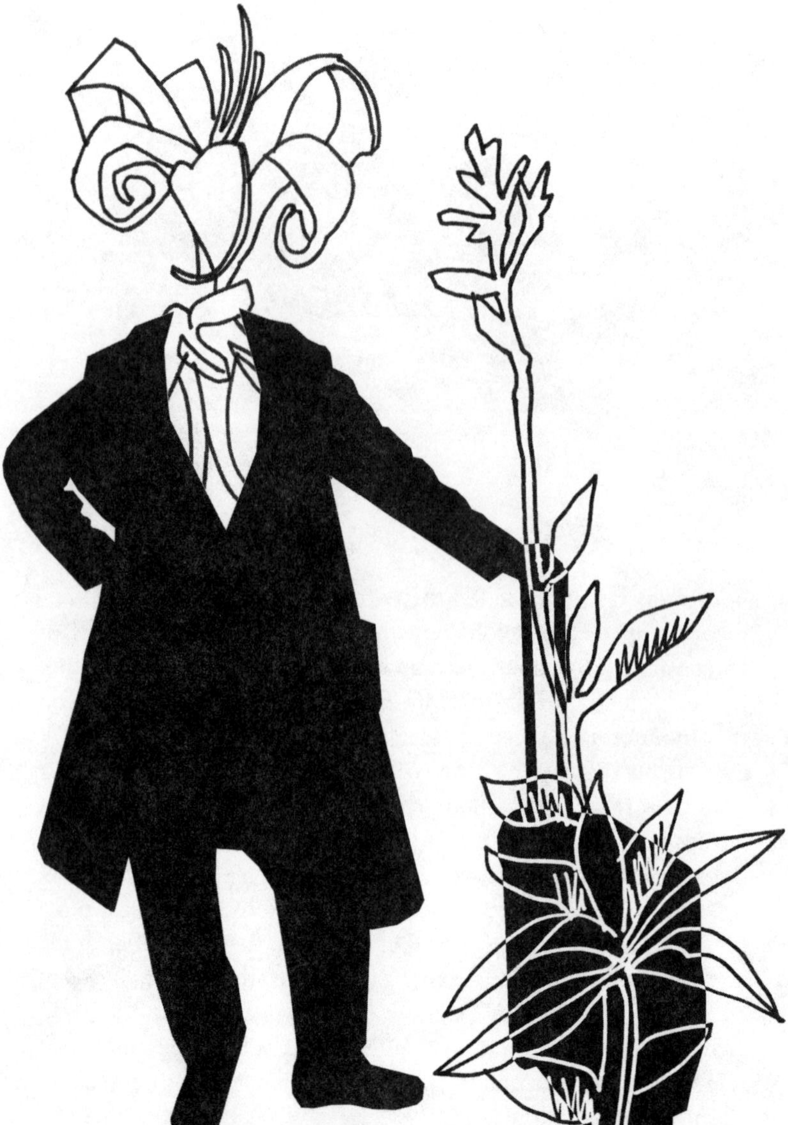

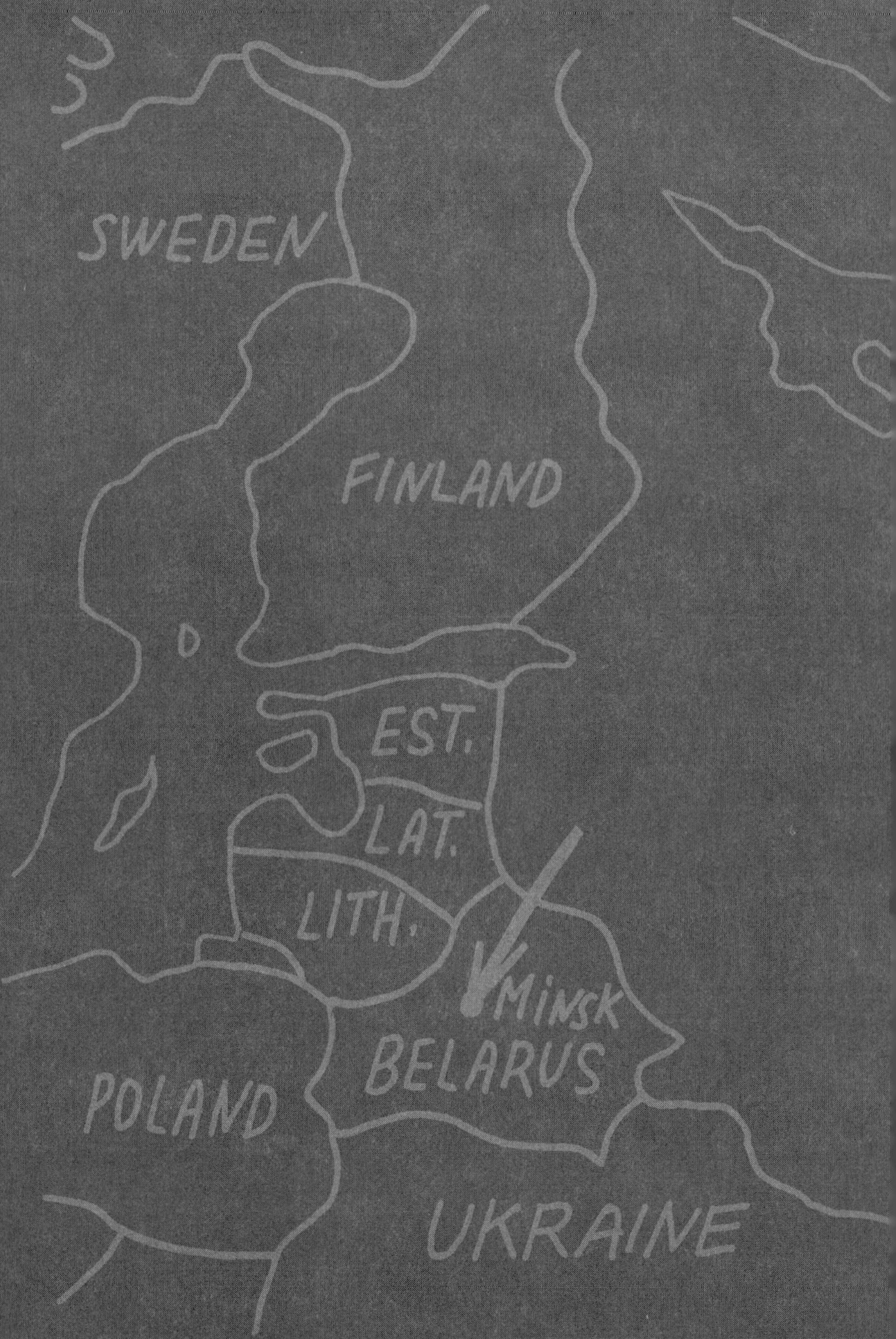
SWEDEN
FINLAND
EST.
LAT.
LITH.
Minsk
BELARUS
POLAND
UKRAINE

A TRIP TO MINSK, 2020

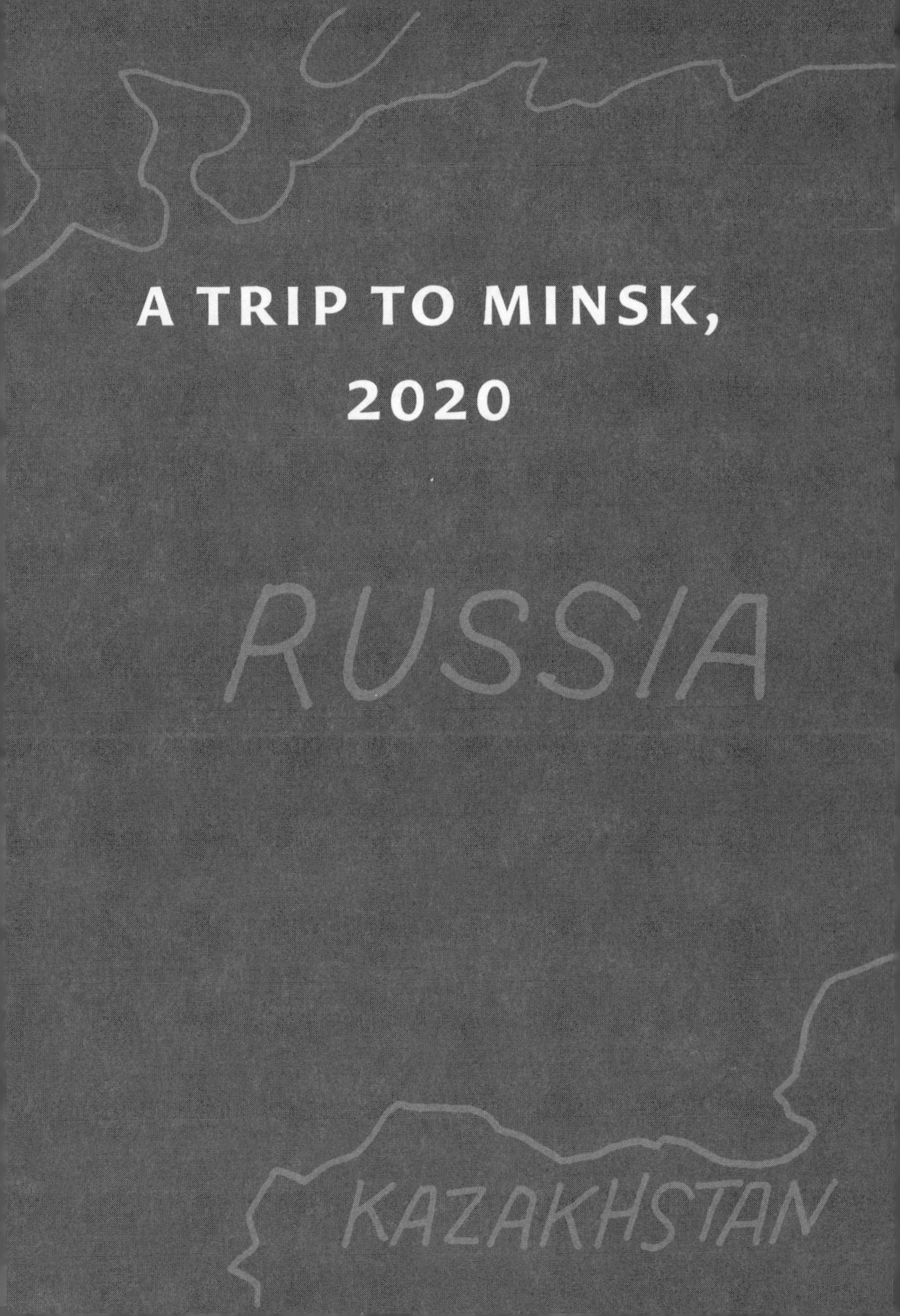
RUSSIA
KAZAKHSTAN

On August 9, 2020, Belarus was swept up in a wave of street protests and other forms of resistance following the contested reelection of Alexander Lukashenko, who had been running the country for twenty-seven years—practically since the fall of the Soviet Union. While those of us in Russia were sitting around posting about the futility of fighting authoritarian regimes, Belarusians had gone out into the streets and braved rubber bullets, stun grenades, and water cannons. Now some of us wanted to go to Belarus ourselves, but the Russian side of the border had been closed since March because of the pandemic.

MONDAY — A BLACK DAY

In Minsk, Saturday was the day of the Women's March; on Sunday, thousands of people went out in the streets to demonstrate, and then on Monday came the arrests and the court dates for those who had protested over the weekend.

Arresting artists—that's new.

She wasn't involved in politics professionally.

I got to Minsk on Monday, September 7, the day the government started arresting activist artists. The artist Nadya Sayapina had been part of a political performance; she was taken from her home.

That same day, the well-known eco-activist Irina Sukhiy was sentenced for participating in an unsanctioned rally. Other activists showed up to the court to support her. Many people wore masks, less because they didn't want to be infected than to protect their identities from the ever-present titushky (hired thugs), a constant feature of every political event in Minsk. Belarusians joke that they've actually beaten the pandemic, because they've managed to put it out of their minds for the moment.

I was able to get into the tiny courtroom, where people were seated in every other chair. But there was nothing to draw there: both the accused and the witness, a police officer, were testifying via Skype. Only the judge could see them, on her laptop.

"We law enforcement officers monitor the streams on Telegram and the social networks," the police officer said. "We went through photos of the Women's March and recognized citizen Sukhiy. I saw a white and red non-government flag and heard anti-government protesters chanting, 'Shame!'"

Irina Sukhiy was sentenced to five days of administrative detention. The following day, Nadya Sayapina got fifteen days in jail.

WOMEN ON THE FRONT LINES OF THE PROTEST MOVEMENT

After Lukashenko disqualified all the male presidential candidates, he felt there was no harm in letting one of their wives run. "She cooked up a nice meat patty and fed the kiddies," he told an interviewer who asked about Svetlana Tikhanovskaya. "The smell of that tasty patty is still in the air, but now she has to go and debate these terrible issues." Belarusians are sure that Tikhanovskaya actually won the election. She has become a symbol of the protest movement.

— We're taking advantage of their stereotype that women are fragile creatures.

"Yesterday I saw a woman lie down on top of a man to protect him while he was getting beat up by enforcers," said N., an activist. At first, the women were not detained with the same kind of brutality as the men. On several occasions, women formed chains of solidarity without any of them getting arrested. Some even brought their children.

Just as in Russia, twentysomethings are especially active at the protests. No one expected this from the generation that grew up under Putin and Lukashenko, but it turned out that having been born in a world without an Iron Curtain—and getting the opportunity to compare the difference between the quality of life in post-Soviet countries and in the West—was enough.

"When I was little, I saw Russia as an interesting, progressive country," Diana said. "But after 2012, it became obvious that you guys were living under your own authoritarian regime."

Vika recalled the events of August 10, which she took part in. "That day, they killed a man on Pushkinskaya Street. Something terrible happened, there was shooting. We hadn't reached the intersection when they started throwing stun grenades. In the courtyard, enforcers chased and caught people and shot at us with rubber bullets. Everything everywhere went off like fireworks until three in the morning. It felt like war."

Diana, 23

We don't want to live any worse than our friends in the West, but in our own country.

In the courtyard, enforcers chased and caught people and shot at us with rubber bullets. Everything everywhere went off like fireworks until three in the morning. It felt like war.

That day, they killed a man on Pushkinskaya Street. Something terrible happened, there was shooting. We hadn't reached the intersection when they started throwing stun grenades.

The main thing psychologists are dealing with right now are feelings of guilt. People think that they're not doing enough for the protests.

If the leadership doesn't change in the coming years, I'm not going to stay in Belarus.

I'll keep walking until the end—until they pick me up.

I'm exhausted, but it's even harder to live under this dictatorship.

—My favorite way to relax is sewing a transgender flag for a rally. Earlier today I found out that a friend I went to the march with yesterday had already been arrested this morning. It was the first time I've cried since all this started.

On Tuesday, September 8, a call went out on the NEXTA Telegram channel for a women's action in support of Maria Kolesnikov, one of the leaders of the opposition, who had just been kidnapped by police. The majority of protest rallies in Minsk are organized spontaneously through Telegram. A crowd of women gathered next to the Komarovsky Market and began to march in the direction of the city center. People stuck their heads out of their windows as the column passed by, and red and white flags appeared.

One of the slogans chanted by the protesters—"We're in power here!"—was conceived in 2012 by the Russian opposition leader Alexey Navalny during anti-government demonstrations in Moscow, which were attended by thousands. The government responded to our peaceful protests with repression, new laws, and stronger censorship.

Suddenly, out of nowhere, giant, dark-green Minsk police vans appeared and stopped next to the marching women. Men in black balaclavas and unmarked khaki uniforms jumped out and started throwing the women into the vans. As someone who lives in Putin's Russia and takes part in protests, I'm not easily shocked by brutality, but I got scared. I ran across the street at a red light and fled. Later, in photos and videos, I saw that the Belarusian women had not tried to run. They formed human chains, ripped off the men's balaclavas, and even attempted to fight their friends out of the men's grasp.

SIGNS OF RESISTANCE

On weekdays, Minsk can seem like a sleepy place where nothing much happens. But if you look closely, it's full of signs of resistance. Anyone can be a leader, and any neighborhood spot can become a locus of protest.

On a street full of half-empty establishments, there's a tiny coffee shop with an incredibly long line out the door. A few days ago, O'Petit had sheltered protesters fleeing the police. One of the officers broke the café's glass door as revenge.

Now people stand in line for up to an hour and a half at a time, just to have a cup of coffee here and leave a generous tip. The guestbook is full of hearts, red and white symbols, and messages like, "May the New Free Belarus be filled with people like the ones who work at this café and those who spend all day standing in line outside of it!"

Людзі ў вязніцы, хто выйшаў на вуліцы, паглядзеў не так. Мы молімся за іх.

People are in jail, the ones who went out in the streets, who looked at someone wrong. We are praying for them. The kind hearts of our people are our strength. We will defeat evil with good.

You can even go to a Catholic church and hear a sermon in support of peaceful protest.

Red and white bouquets lie at the exit of the Pushkinskaya subway station. In August, a peaceful protester died here during a demonstration. Now there's a spontaneous people's memorial that is constantly being taken down by police. In the ten minutes it took me to draw it, five people stopped by with fresh bouquets. Drivers of passing cars honked at them and people waved from the buses.

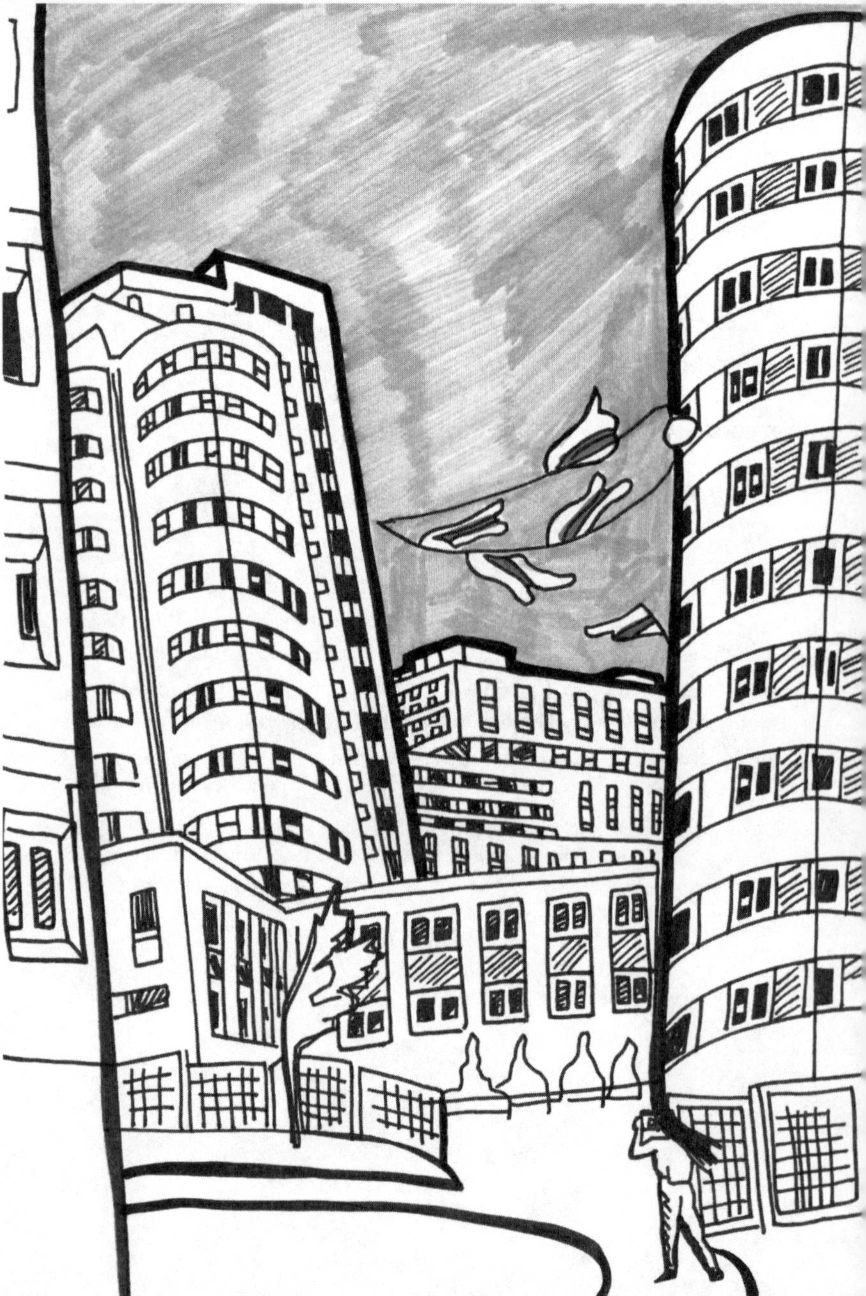

Flags wave like kites over the Cascade apartment complex.

"Most of the people who live here are young and progressive. They're the ones who put out the flags," one building resident explained to me. "When the police tear them down, our people get them back up right away."

In Minsk, people even arrange their laundry to resemble the flag, hanging it out—white, red, white. "The police's main task right now," Minskers joke, "is taking down all the red and white ribbons people are tying on all the fences."

A new form of resistance has emerged: "protest courtyards." The people who live in these courtyards meet to discuss what is happening, hold concerts, organize flash mobs, put up protest graffiti, and project videos. The most well-known "protest courtyard" is called the Courtyard of Changes.

The graffiti on the transformer box in the Courtyard of Changes depicts two Minsk DJs who played Viktor Tsoi's cult anthem "We're Waiting for Change" at a pro-government rally. They were held in jail for ten days. "We're Waiting for Change" is a seminal work from my youth, from the last days of the Soviet Union. The fact that this song still drives authorities crazy shows that the final farewell with the Soviet past is only now taking place.

I was in a cab headed to the Courtyard of Changes when my friends texted to say that the police had just painted over the mural. But by the time I got there, building residents had almost finished repainting it. "This is the sixth time they've painted over it, and we always put it up again right away," they told me, laughing.

All of us know what we're doing on Saturday.
Taking the streets!

TRIAL OF THE ILLEGAL STRIKE

On Friday, September 11, I was drawing at the Minsk Regional Courthouse, where they were hearing the case against the strike committee of Belaruskali, the largest enterprise in Belarus. Belaruskali's workers had been charged with holding an illegal strike. There was no legal precedent for a case of this kind in Belarus.

Like many other large companies in Belarus, Belaruskali belongs to the government, which is more threatened by strikes than by protests.

While we waited for the proceedings to start, men in black balaclavas came into the courtroom and grabbed several women who had come to support the strikers. The court bailiffs stood by, doing nothing to stop them. The women were pushed into a minibus without a license plate and driven away in an unknown direction.

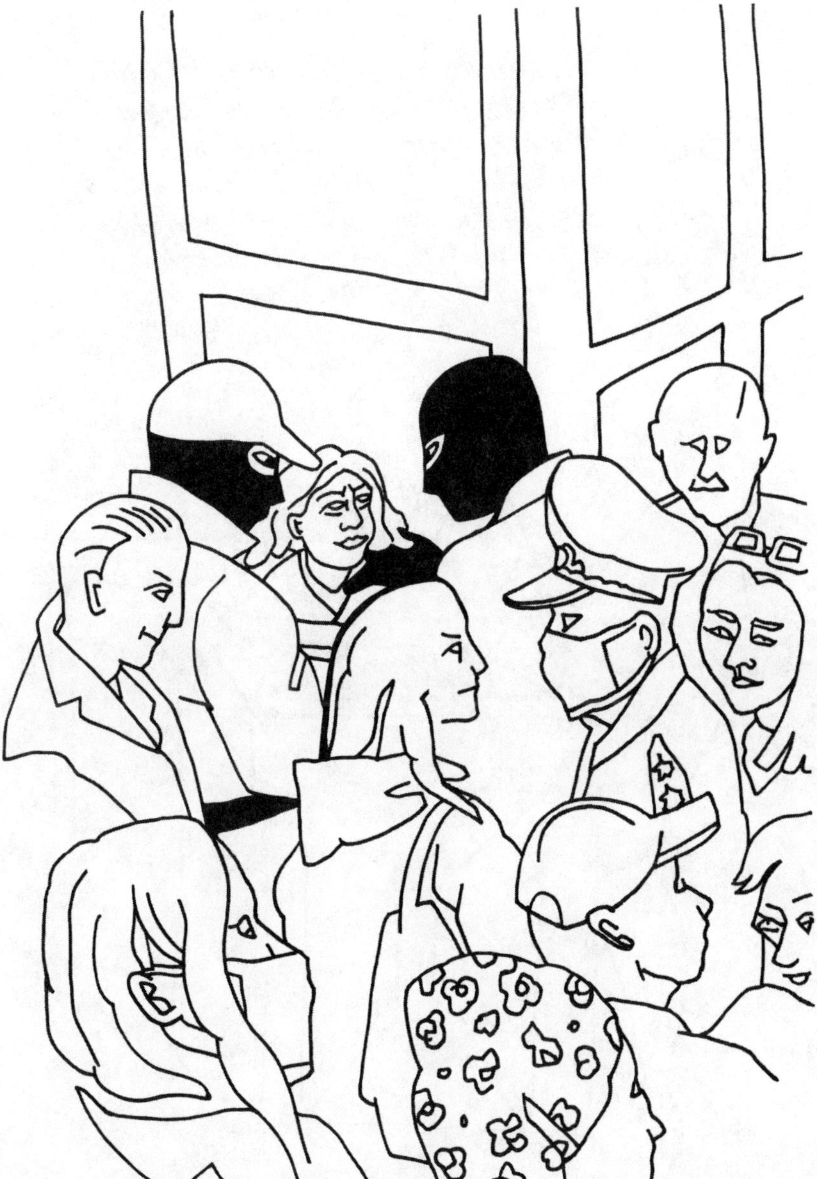

–A strike may be carried out no later than three months from the date of the failure to reach an agreement between the sides of a collective bargaining dispute according to the conciliation committee regulations on collective bargaining disputes. Workers are required to submit notice to their employers two weeks prior to striking.
Prosecutor

-I can confirm that no meetings were held for creating the strike committee.
Plaintiff's! Lawyer
Deputy of the General Director
-It wasn't a meeting—everyone was just yelling at the director.

The defendant was Belaruskali's strike committee, represented in court by Sergey Shitz, the committee's former cochairman. "There was a massive mopping-up operation taking place in the city. Workers were beaten," he said, describing what had happened following the presidential election in Soligorsk, where Belaruskali is located.

— People took off their shirts and showed their injuries from the beatings. They made political demands.

The workers' main demands were that the presidential elections be deemed void, that charges be pressed against Alexander Lukashenko, and that all political prisoners be freed.

The workers had promised to strike indefinitely, but the majority of them returned to work within several days. Sergey Shitz said he considered this a betrayal.

— The strike committee represented the interests of between six and seven thousand workers who signed up to strike. Our demand was that we deal with the genocide of our own people.

— Did the administration figure out why a portion of the workers still haven't come back to work?

— I don't know why some of the workers haven't returned yet. Their reasons may very well be respectable.

LAWYER

Deputy of the General Director

It felt like it wasn't just the strike organizers who were on trial, but also the company administration, which had failed to immediately quash the protest. During questioning, the judge collected a list of the names of the workers who had actively supported the strike and had not yet returned to work. The court declared the strike illegal.

THE LONG-AWAITED WEEKEND

Toward the end of the week, word went around Telegram that on Saturday the "loudest women's march yet" would take place on Freedom Square. I was more interested in drawing than demonstrating, so I got there early and sat down at an outdoor café with a view of the square. Small groups of women slowly strolled around, dressed in red and white. At the appointed time, they quickly formed a crowd. Immediately, unmarked minibuses pulled up and men in balaclavas jumped out and started grabbing the women.

A woman and her son watched from a neighboring table:

"Those gangsters are back..."

"But Mama, I thought they were policemen."

"Now they're gangsters."

I tried warning women who were hurrying to get to the square:

"Girls, hold on! They're grabbing everyone over there! Go around the other side!"

"If they're rounding up our friends, that's exactly where we need to go."

The square slowly filled up with police vans; it looked like the set for a war movie. The women formed a column and simply began to march down another route.

The following day they held a March of Heroes, one of those Sunday demonstrations that thousands of people attended, the kind I'd jealously seen in photos back at home in depressing Moscow. I'd wanted so badly to find myself inside that picture.

Early on Sunday morning, I looked out the window where I was staying and saw the police vans and unmarked buses convoying downtown to surround the city center. Fifteen minutes later, as I was jumping into a taxi, soldiers were already marching into the courtyard.

In the afternoon, I headed toward the Nyamiha subway station, where protesters were collecting.

The violent arrests began as soon as people started unfurling their flags. Some ran into cafés, others into stores, but the enforcers managed to drag some of them out. Many businesses had closed their doors ahead of time.

Along with hundreds of others, I found myself cut off from the main crowd which was now moving into the neighborhood around the Cascade apartment complex. By then, the authorities had shut down the subway and cut off mobile internet. We were trying to catch up with the crowd. The most unpleasant part was crossing a long bridge over the railroad. I remembered stories I'd heard about how, the previous weekend, people had jumped into the cold river to get away from the police.

That day, protesters reached the elite suburb of Drozdy, home to one of Lukashenko's residences as well as the country homes of his close associates. I couldn't take the pressure again and turned back halfway.

THERE are police vans with water cannons waiting for us on Frunzenskaya.
Mama, I didn't know the bridge was so long. I can't do it, I can't anymore!

Instead of the two weeks I'd planned to spend in Minsk, one was enough for me. I was hoping to get back to Moscow without any unwanted adventures. The border on the way back was open to those with Russian passports, but the other passengers on the private coach bus I took back to Moscow were all Belarusian and not allowed in because of the pandemic—which is why the driver drove around along the border, hoping to cross through a country road. The other passengers read Telegram channels and discussed Sunday's rally. One man assured everyone that people in the know had just called him and told him that tomorrow Russia would bring in its army and put down the protests. I watched the black sky through the window and thought about how, in the course of history, it wasn't that important what Putin or Lukashenko were going to do now.... The river of time moves forward, even if it's moving slowly, washing away the traces of everything Soviet like so much flotsam.

KREMLIN

MOSCOW: A BATTLE OF THE GENERATIONS, 2021

The Covid winter of 2020 was remarkably snowy. There were deep frosts in January and, as if rhyming with the icy snow drifts, all social life came to a standstill.

Opposition leader Alexei Navalny, who had been poisoned with the nerve agent Novichok in August, was going through a course of treatment in Berlin. In neighboring Belarus, thanks to Putin's support, Lukashenko had managed to put down a revolution. A new law was passed in Russia according to which anyone who published any kind of political statement, in the press or on their social media, and who received any kind of support from abroad, could be declared a foreign agent and put on a list. The forced branding of "foreign agent," the fines, the state's total financial control—anyone subjected to this would find their professional future over.

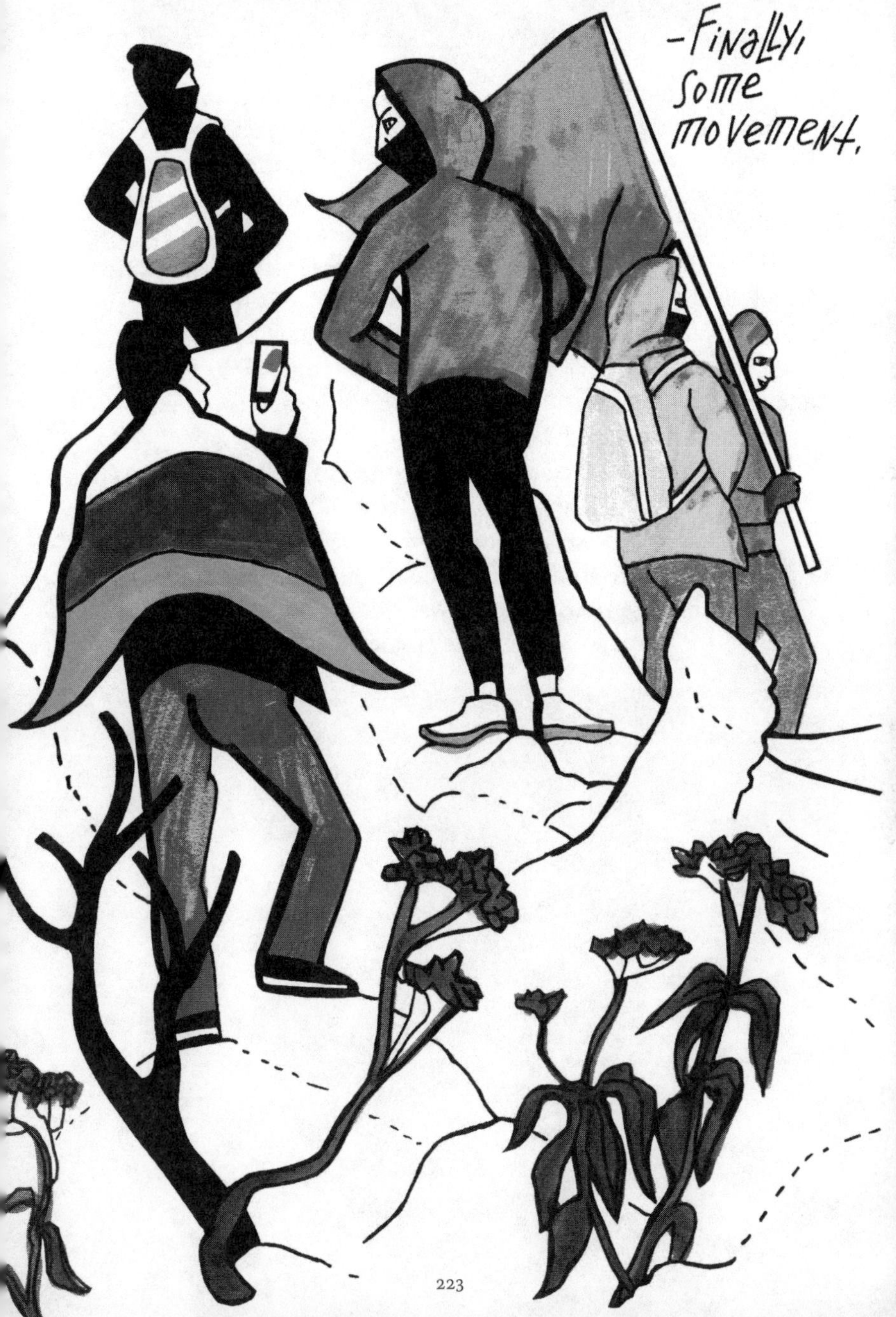
-Finally, some movement.

2021 came in with a bang: the news that Navalny was coming back to Russia. On the eve of his return, the politician called the men who were supposed to have killed him and one of them, sure that he was talking to an FSB chief, revealed the details of his poisoning. On January 17, Vnukovo Airport, where Navalny's airplane was supposed to land, suddenly stopped accepting incoming flights. The plane had to land in Sheremetyevo, where Navalny was immediately arrested on charges related to the Yves Rocher case, which began in 2013. Navalny posted his YouTube investigation into Putin's secret 100-billion-ruble palace once he was already in the president's custody.

We sat glued to the amazing adventures of Aleksei Navalny as if they were a movie. It was more addictive than Netflix. The sparks of his daring had landed on us, too—people were regaining interest in Russia again. Navalny's call to demonstrate against Putin's regime on January 23 gave us a choice: were we going to remain passive viewers, or would we become the protagonists of this show?

JANUARY 23

In the lead-up to January 23, one of my neighbors came over to see me a couple of times. He was a pretty apolitical guy—the last time he'd been to a demonstration was in 2012. We decided to go together. We talked about how many people would lose their jobs, get expelled from college—how many would get fined, injured, arrested for several nights, or even end up in prison.

—It feels scary to go, but I'll go.

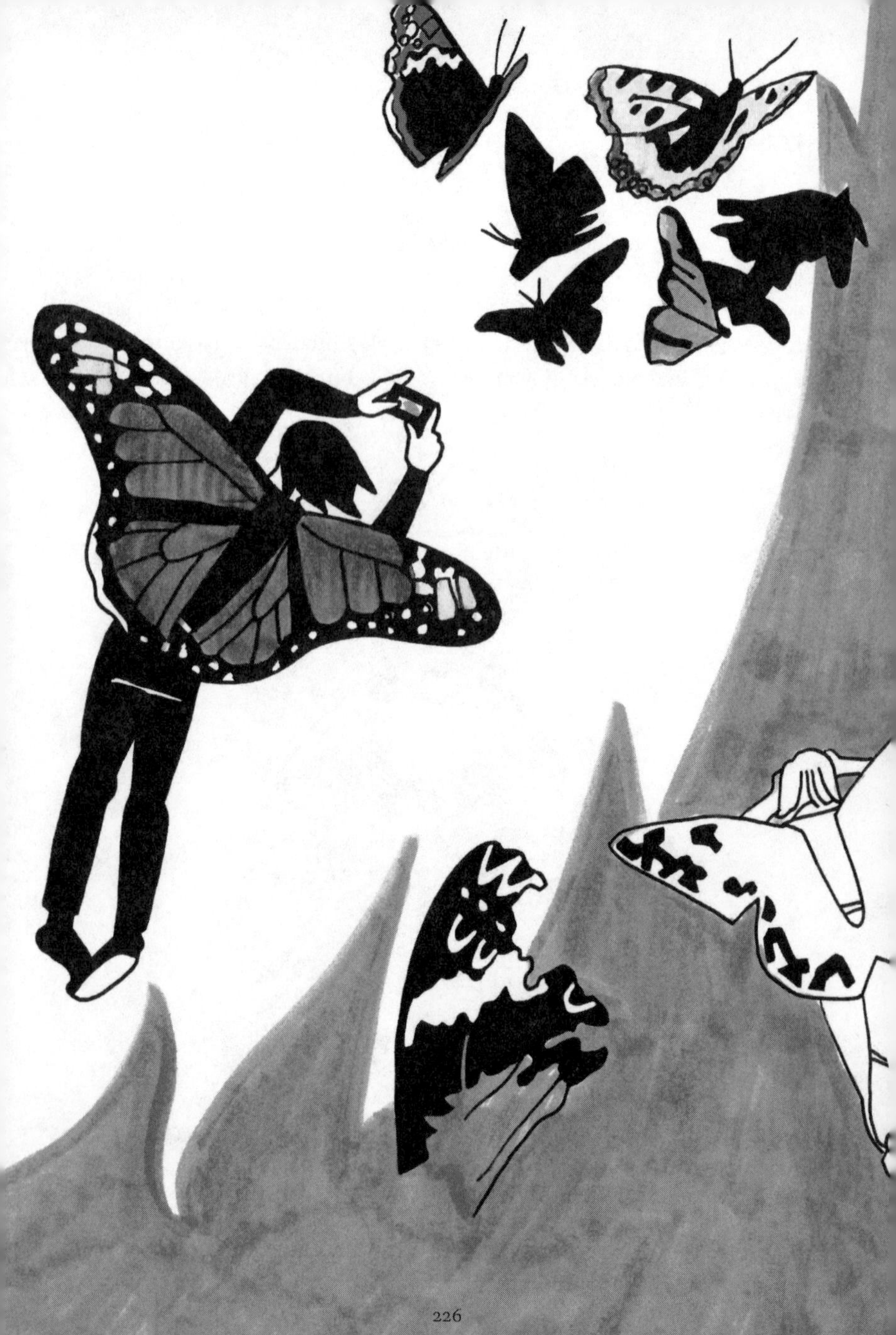

I called my friends and acquaintances. Everyone felt the energy of the impending events, and that energy drew us in like moths to a flame.

Many wanted to go not because they wanted to save Navalny, but because they couldn't not go—the historical whirlwind was sucking them in.

Analysts promised that only teenagers would come to the demonstration, the ones whose anti-Putin and pro-Navalny videos were filling up TikTok. But the first people we saw as we approached weren't even teenagers—they were just kids making snowmen.

After that, a young man and woman with posters grabbed my attention. The woman's poster read, "What me and the other girls dream about: 1) $ 2) love 3) a car 4) for Putin to die tonight." The man's poster said, "I'm not afraid of grandpa in his bunker." There was something weird on his forehead, but when I looked closer I saw that it was a headband with a symbol on it. It was a cosplay from Naruto, the cult manga series about teens with magical powers who have to fight adult demons. Everything all around us was filling up with symbols hinting at a battle of the generations: the younger, the mobile, and the new vs. the older, the ossified, and the Soviet.

IZVESTIA
WHAT ME
AND THE OTHER girls
dream about:
1) $ 2) ♥ 3)
4) FOR PUTIN
to die tonight
I'm not afraid
of grandpa
in his bunk

I spent a few hours at the demonstration. I didn't try to get close to the monument to Aleksandr Pushkin, where people were being violently arrested. Standing in the crowd, watching the beautiful youth who wished for the best, it felt like a swarm of colorful birds had landed on the snow and that there was nothing at all in common between them and the approaching black phalanx of riot police.

JUST AS LONG AS THERE'S NO WAR

Navalny's office planned for the next demonstration to take place on January 31. The police completely cordoned off downtown Moscow ahead of time and on the 31st none of the subway stations in the center were open. I decided not to put myself under the truncheons that day.

The police were especially brutal: they didn't just beat people with their clubs—they also used Tasers and tear gas, and one of the police officers pointed a gun at the protesters.

That evening, I got a text from a friend who had emigrated to Berlin.

"Hey Vika! Are you on the outside?"

"I didn't go today."

"I see."

Sorry, friend, no firsthand recap of the show today.

The following day, I overheard the conversation of a group of senior citizens who were sitting on a bench in my courtyard. The old man told his neighbor that "in other countries, they only have sanctioned demonstrations," and responded that she'd seen on TV how "the police were giving demonstrators tea and cookies." How many conversations like this one have I heard in my life? During the vote to amend the Russian constitution in the summer of 2020, I drew at the polling places, and it was always the old folks who were most eager to talk to me. "There's no way to survive on our pensions," they said, but "we voted for Putin." Why? "Just as long as there's no war."

These people were completely traumatized by hunger and social collapse. Those born after World War II, however, can relate to the president's idea that we need to build an impassable wall between ourselves and our enemies throughout the rest of the world. If they ever began to entertain the idea that the world is actually an open and friendly place, something terrible was bound to happen: it would turn out that the unbearable struggle their lives amounted to had been a needless sacrifice. I suspect that the Soviet regime persisted for as long as it did not because people believed in the ultimate triumph of communism, but because they were terrified of the enemies at the gates.

ALEXEY NAVALNY'S VERDICT

Alexey Navalny's verdict was handed down on February 2. So many journalists from leading publications wanted to get into the courtroom that it didn't even make sense for an independent journalist and artist to try.

The streets around the Moscow City Court, where the trial was taking place, had been cordoned off by the police ahead of time and neighborhood bus lines were rerouted. I don't live very far from the Court, so I decided to walk as far as I could to see precisely where ordinary life was transitioning into a scene from a horror film.

I walked down Bolshaya Cherkizovskaya Street, which was filled with people running their errands. What's going on here? I wondered. One man put his life on the line trying to move the immovable political system. Risking injuries, fines, and jail time, almost 150,000 thousand people from all across the country went out into the streets. Meanwhile, what do the rest of the 146 million people living in Russia feel?

It looked like there'd been a terrorist attack next to the Preobrazhenskaya Ploshchad metro station. There was an extremely long line of police vans, police cars, and every other kind of police vehicle imaginable. Groups of law enforcement agents walked back and forth. They were entirely covered by various kinds of shields and defensive devices—they looked like lizards, with black scales. Their black visors made it impossible to see their faces.

Passengers getting off the buses and people sitting at the stop pretended not to notice the apocalyptic scene. The former were trying to get out of there as quickly as they could, and the latter were focused on their phones. After a while, the buses stopped coming. Then people started talking to one another.

"I don't watch the news, right? They're so serious. Why do we have to suffer?"

"How am I supposed to get home now? I'm hungry!"

The buses aren't running.
I don't have money for a cab.
What's going on here?

Several angry old women had been standing at the bus stop for a long time. A woman came up to them to ask why the buses weren't running. "What don't you understand? They've brought in the greenhorns!" the angriest one said.

The police walking past us looked like greenhorns to me, too, and I was happy that not all the old people were Putin supporters. But the old woman continued, "It's all because of those puppies defending Navalny in court."

The angry old women went off somewhere. Only one tiny grandma was left, preaching, "What's happening—all because of that one idiot! How am I supposed to get home now?"

I got angry with her and said with a laugh, "Ask your president to help you."

"He'll help me alright. As long as I get on that one," she said, pointing to the police bus parked in front of the bus stop.

"So maybe the youth aren't wrong in not wanting to go back to Soviet times?"

"You don't know the USSR. We worked hard, we did any job we could. But there were free clinics, safety . . ."

"And what do we have now?"

"None of that. I'm 82 and I have to walk home twenty stops. Nobody needs us old folk. Nobody cares about us. But we were the ones who won the war . . ."

I wanted to call her a taxi, but my phone was dead and I didn't have any cash. No cab would have been able to come down these cordoned-off streets anyway. Dragging her shopping cart through the snow, the old woman walked off with a sigh.

That was the day that they sentenced Navalny to two years and eight months of prison.

MOSCOW: LIFE ON THE ISLAND, 2021

After the January 2021 protests, which ended with another assault on the opposition, life in Moscow came to a standstill again. Things froze so much that in the spring I started planting flowers in the little front garden outside my apartment building and spending hours drawing plants, like I used to when I was little. On the other side of Moscow, I discovered a plot that one of the residents of a neighboring high-rise had transformed into a real garden. The amateur gardener was a young man named Sergey. He planted his garden so that every month, it changed color and shape. During the pandemic, it was scary to use public transportation in Moscow, since people tended to wear masks on only their chins, so I would take a cab to draw an important event: another change in the garden.

I would sit in front of the flowerbed in my folding chair drawing daffodils and tulips with their coarse leaves. Then, at the height of summer, flowering rose bushes. Then, toward the end of August, the magical, baroque-looking phloxes and lilies. When I realized that all those demonstrations hadn't taught me to be sensitive, I decided I needed to learn from the flowers. People would stop behind me and watch all the time, sighing, "Lord, how beautiful!" They didn't mean my drawings—they meant Sergey's garden.

ACTIVISTS

There were parliamentary elections scheduled for September. Ten years earlier, mass demonstrations had been set off by similar elections and proceeded for a year. I'd drawn at all of them. In the intervening years, the majority of my friends who had participated in those protests had emigrated to the West. Those who stayed in Russia and had remained activists were eagerly awaiting the September events.

Among the Moscow candidates, two seemed progressive: the popular feminist Alena Popova and the leftist activist Mikhail Lobanov.

Alena Popova, 38. Criminal justice attorney. Founder of the organization TyNeOdna (which translates as You'reNotAlone), which supports survivors of domestic abuse. Co-author of an anti–domestic violence bill. The main points of her platform were: passing a law against domestic violence and repealing the repressive censorship laws.

—Our campaign slogan is: "Don't just survive—thrive."

Mikhail Lobanov, 37. Moscow State University professor, PhD in math and physics. Defends the rights of students and teachers, one of the founders of a union called University Solidarity. Participated in several environmental campaigns. Communist Party candidate.

Mikhail Lobanov's platform: progressive tax reform, support for free healthcare and education, protecting the natural and urban environment, lowering the retirement age, and raising pensions.

— We're against inequality, which why our slogan is: "A future for all, not just the few."

More than anything, Lobanov resembles one of the Soviet statues at the university's entrance. He's like a young bronze scientist who has left behind his book, jumped off his pedestal, and headed out to fight the Putin regime.

Alena Popova was a candidate in my district, Preobrazhenskoye. I visited her campaign headquarters several times—it was close to my house. It was mostly young women working there. I tagged along with one of them as she roamed through the streets and collected signatures for an anti-domestic violence bill and encouraged people to vote in the State Duma elections.

After signing the petition, one young woman told us that she had recently become the target of sexual harassment and she didn't know what to do.

Another woman told us about the kinds of issues she's concerned about after she signed the petition:

Mikhail Lobanov's campaign headquarters were in Ramenky, on the Moscow outskirts. At the end of August, Lobanov organized a subbotnik, a Saturday clean-up at a local riverbank. The tiny river flowed through the bottom of a set of deep ravines. They were completely covered in trash.

Wandering through a ravine filled with thick undergrowth, at first I couldn't find anyone. Finally, I saw two activists in rubber boots standing in the middle of a heap of rags, bags, bottles, old shoes, wires, boxes, and other garbage. "This is traumatizing for me to look at—let's get the hubcaps instead," one of the activists said. "OK, gathering hubcaps is helpful, too," the other one replied. At that point Mikhail Lobanov appeared out of the tall weeds alongside Kirill Medvedev, the famous poet, translator, activist, and singer in the punk group Arkady Kots. They were dragging along some hubcaps and a half-rotten rug. They reminded me of Neanderthals bearing tusks and animal pelts.

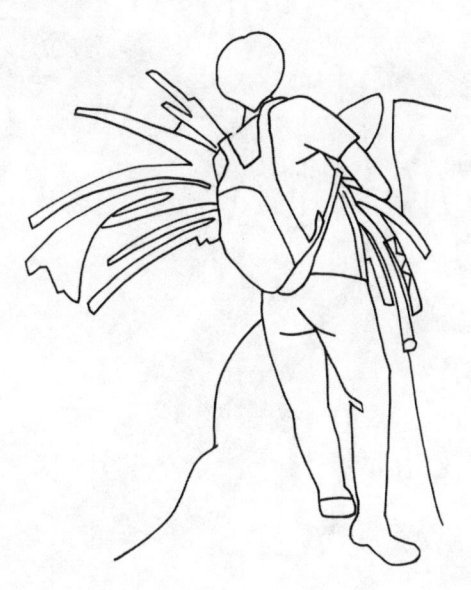

The activists collected twenty bags' worth of garbage. Then, like a gang of Sisyphuses, they scrambled their way up the filthy cliffside with their garbage bags. It was clear that if we wanted to clean up this place, we'd either need to organize hundreds of subbotniks like this, or change our political regime.

I kept seeking out events that would feel representative of political life in Moscow in 2021. Some friends told me about one of the organizers working with Lobanov, an activist named Dima Morozov, who was currently making clay figurines for an Arkady Kots protest music video. Why not draw a young activist working in clay?

Dima lived with a young gender studies scholar named Sasha Talaver—they had recently met in the leftist organization RSD, which they were both involved with. I went over to see them.

Dima and his beloved sat making the figurines: here was Putin, here were police offers in the form of dogs and pigs. The music video was supposed to weave medieval fairytale themes with our current terrible reality. "What do you think, could you face repression for your clay things?" I asked. "I don't even know," Dima said. "There's a line in the song that goes, 'And we'll hang the king from a branch,' and I'm here making Putin."

Dima was born and grew up in Izhevsk, the capital of Udmutria, one of the poorest and most disadvantaged republics in Russia. He was raised by his grandparents, an engineer and a schoolteacher. He'd always disliked the rich because when he was still in school, he was faced with the problem that, in his words, "There were rich shitheads, and then there were poor kids who had to make excuses for why they couldn't afford to go on school trips." When he was 16, Dima and his friends organized a socialist movement called Iskra, which was around for three years. At one point, Dima was looking through an old issue of the anarchist newspaper *Volya* and came upon a work of graphic reportage I published, "Chronicles of Resistance," about the 2012 protests in Moscow. After that, Iskra's agitational materials took on the same black and red. In January 2021, during the pro-Navalny protests, leftist activists in Izhevsk, including Dima, organized a demonstration of five thousand people.

Like many other people in their twenties, Dima idealizes the Soviet Union, where he never lived. But when I asked him to sketch an ideal future for Russia, he described a modern European state. "The leftist idea isn't worth anything if it doesn't provide people happiness and comfort," he said. "You're living your life, and your kids and your relatives are, too." The word "comfort" came up in all of my conversations with people in their twenties. And if that word has finally pushed out of their minds the classic Soviet concepts of feats, heroes, and grand obligations, maybe material reality finally has a chance of rising to the level of the new mentality.

I'd had September 4 marked on my calendar a long time—this was the day that the opposition had been allowed to hold two whole events!

One of them was a protest against the law on foreign agents, which had been disguised as a rally with the opposition candidates to the State Duma. About fifty people showed up.

I noticed a woman who was carrying around a cardboard cutout of famous opposition figure Yulia Galyamina. The woman turned out to be her daughter. A court had forbidden Galyamina from attending political events, so now she was participating as a cardboard cutout.

After the protest was over and everyone started to scatter, I heard someone call my name. It was a foreign journalist who had done a story with me for Swiss television before the pandemic. "Hey!" she shouted. "I thought everyone had left Russia already. It's good that at least some people are still here."

That same day, under the guise of a meet and greet with legislators, the communists had a rally "for honest and clean elections." While everyone was waiting for it to begin, an old woman began reciting some political poems she'd written. The crowd liked what they heard.

> Where can regular people go?
> They always send the cops.
>
> Another order, one more law,
> Putin is our boss.
>
> We have to reinstate the past,
> Fight to fulfill our vow,
> Get back everything Stalinist—
> There's nothing better now!

There was a fair amount of young people in the crowd in addition to the elderly communists. It seemed that they wanted to take part in at least some kind of protest and out of a lack of options they came here.

On the eve of the elections, I went to a meet and greet with Alena Popova in my neighborhood. Around ten well-dressed young women showed up. It was getting dark and it was very cold. The people coming out of the subway refused to take the informational materials from the activists and hurried home. After asking a few questions, the fashion girls went home, too. Popova and the young women from her office were left standing alone on the empty, windblown street, with just me and a couple of foreign correspondents. I felt like I had found myself in a tiny town at the edge of the earth, rather than in the capital standing next to one of the most progressive candidates for State Duma. Popova invited us to go to the nearest park to look for potential voters. We ran through an almost empty park—the only people there were lying down on the benches, extremely drunk. At last we found a man who was having trouble standing. He wasn't interested in the elections, but he was happy to tell us his sad story. Popova and the activists comforted him, saying that life would get better.

Most importantly, don't drink. We can tell that you're a strong-willed person.

The elections took place between September 17 and September 19. In Moscow and a few other regions, voters could either go to their polling place in person or cast a ballot online. The opposition candidates asked voters not to vote using government websites.

I spent September 19 at Mikhail Lobanov's headquarters. Dima was calling voters reminding them that today was their last chance to vote. One after another, activists showed up to the office to get documents that would allow them to be election observers. In the evening I headed home, while the people in the campaign offices and the observers continued working through the night, hoping to interfere with the falsification of the election results.

After the initial count at the polling places, Mikhail Lobanov was ahead of the United Russia candidate by twelve thousand votes. In most of Moscow's districts, candidates that had been put forth by the administration were losing.

The vote counting stretched unexpectedly into the morning of September 20. According to the results of electronic voting, the United Russia candidate was ahead of Lobanov by twenty thousand votes. After the results of electronic voting were announced, it became clear that across all the districts in Moscow, United Russia candidates and other pro-government candidates had won by large margins.

On September 20, communists opposed to the election results held an unsanctioned rally on Pushkin Square. A few hundred people came. I saw Dima and Sasha in the crowd, shouting "Lobanov!"

"Do you see? The sky is weeping over the election results in the Russian Federation," a communist said from the stage.

In subsequent days, there were police raids across Moscow. They had reviewed their security footage and figured out who had attended to the protest and came to their homes. Many people got several nights in jail.

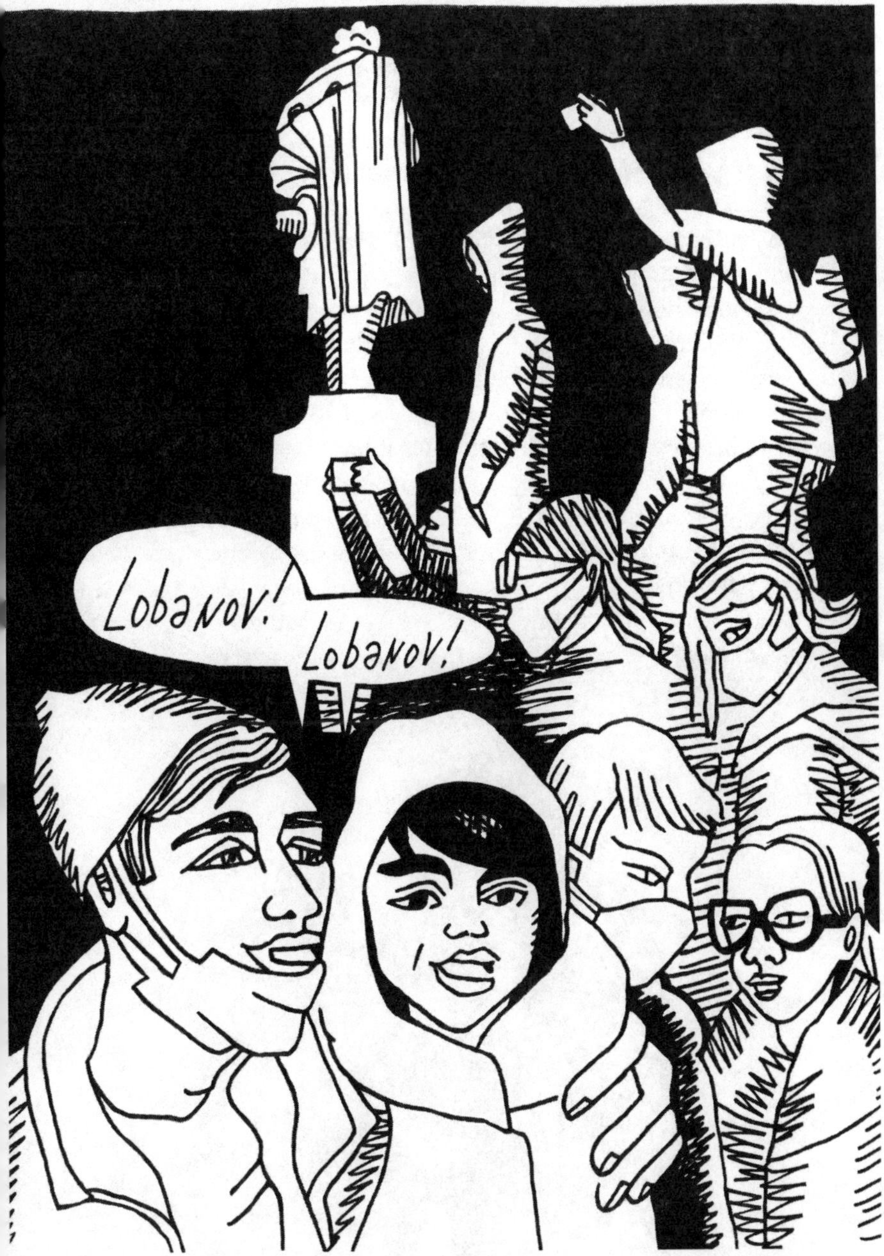
Lobanov!
Lobanov!

October and November passed without anything much having taken place, and then it was December. Moscow was covered in snow—snow that would, as usual, stay on the ground until the middle of March. I spent most of my time at home going through the materials I'd gathered during the campaigns and elections. There wasn't that much. I decided to meet up with Dima to see how his pigs and dogs had turned out.

Dima showed me a pig on a horse, a couple of dog policemen, and Putin in a Monomakh hat. He said that the guys from Arkady Kots decided that Putin should only appear in the teaser and to use an abstract figure in the music video itself. I was happy that Dima wouldn't have to go to jail over claymation.

In the time since we'd last seen each other, Dima had been expelled from the RSD. His former collaborators from Izhevsk had accused him of authoritarianism and harassment. "I want to step away from politics," Dima said. "It's been a source of anger and condescension in my life. I want to focus on art: making rap and claymation. It's so cool. I'm having the best time ever."

The thing that Dima was happiest about was his relationship with Sasha. "Sasha completely transformed my worldview, I've started feeling a lot better about people," he said.

—Love is the kind of thing where even if you're a slave in ancient Rome or you live in a hellhole like Russia, you can still have a good time.

As we said goodbye, Dima asked me what a real artist should be like. I told him that an artist isn't someone who chases after events in the outside world, but whose internal perceptions are themselves the main event.

If someone had asked me this question a year earlier, I would have offered a totally different answer. Back then, I identified as an artist-journalist and chased after political developments in order to hook up to them as if they were some big, external power source. Between 2012 and 2016, there were a lot of interesting political processes to follow in Russia, and I had managed to capture them. But what is an artist-journalist supposed to do when there aren't any major events?

Why not try writing about something other than protests and the activists who participate in them? For example, art and the artists who make it. I used to believe that artists from the Second World were supposed to make political art about social inequality and that creating one's own world was a privilege only available to artists from wealthy countries. But this, I realized, had just been my personal conviction—one that I had the power to change.

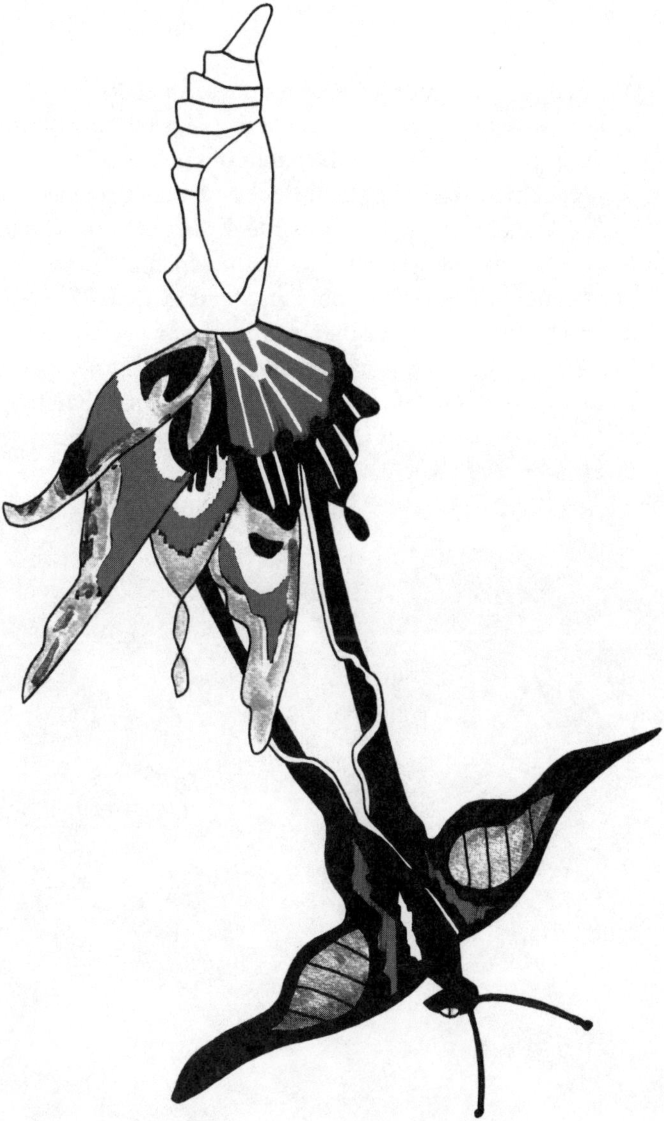

ARTISTS

My first visit was to Marina Antonova, an artist who draws red rabbits. Marina rents an apartment on the outskirts of town in one of those gray high-rises on the banks of the Moscow River.

For some reason, her fifth-floor apartment smelled like a log cabin. The narrow hallway was filled with old furniture and the floor was covered by a long rug, all of which reminded me of my grandmother's house. The room that Marina used as her studio had a strange, spiral-shaped light fixture—the owner of the apartment had had it custom-made, for whatever reason. The wooden window frames were very old, so there was a draft. Marina's paintings, filled with fantastical animals and birds and views of a gloomy, fairytale forest, were everywhere.

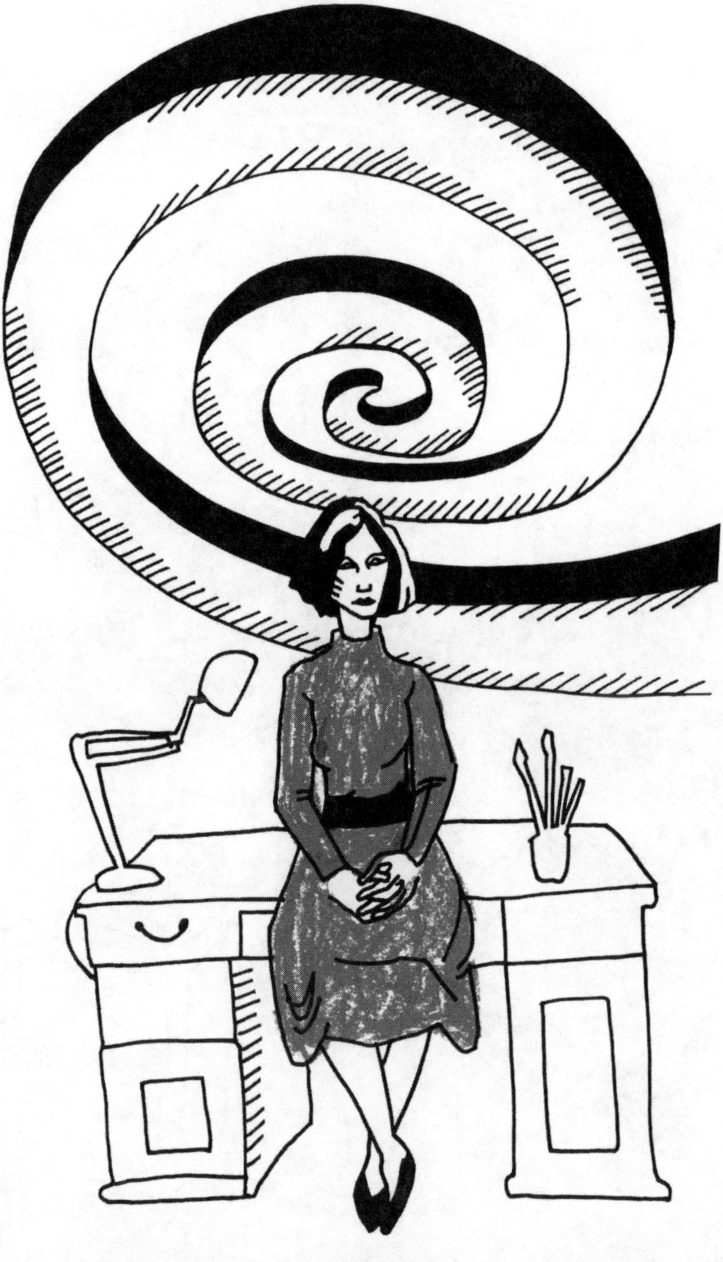

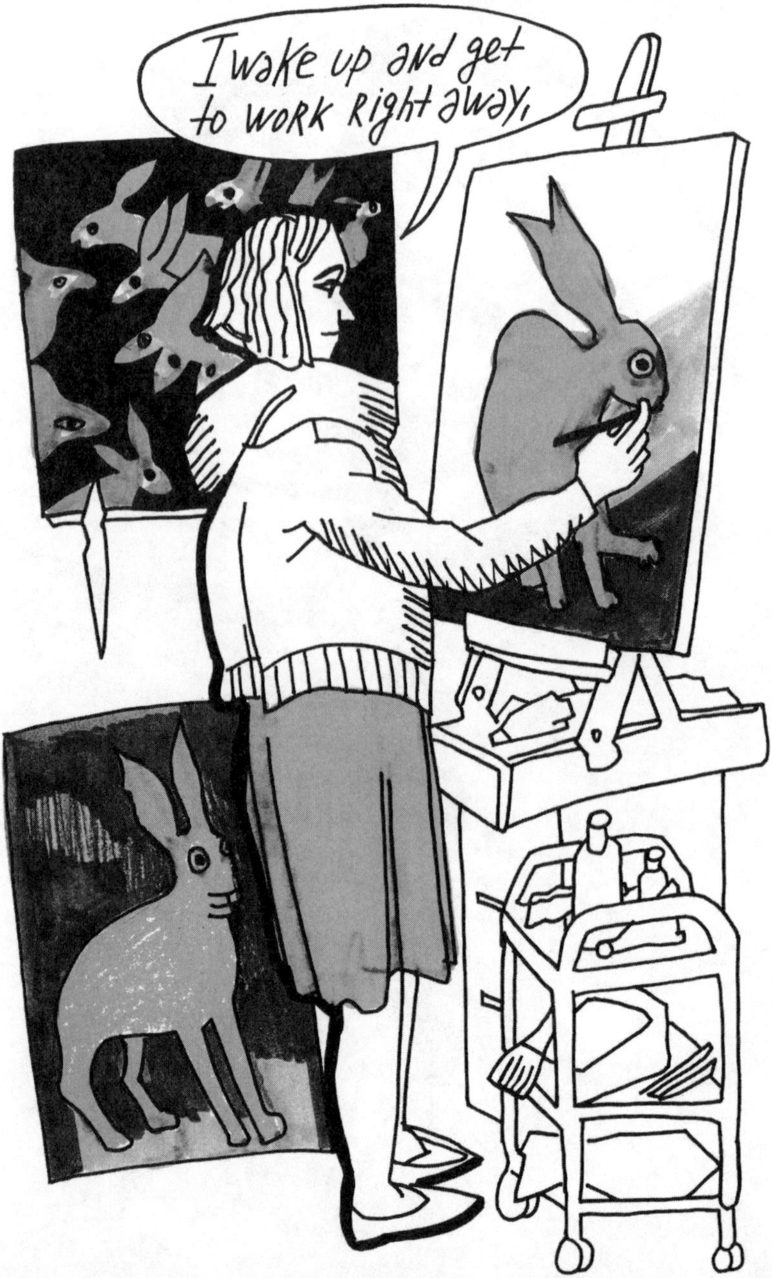
I wake up and get to work right away.

I asked Marina to tell me about her paintings. "My rabbits have snake eyes, cat paws, and lion claws," she began. "They're red because red is the bravest and most provocative color. When I started drawing red rabbits, my taste in clothes changed. People born in the provinces like I was think that you have to blend into the high-rises in the city, the gray reality. I used to wear gray, brown, and black. After I started doing the rabbits, I began wearing red, yellow, orange, and pink. Now I feel safe."

Marina sells her paintings on Instagram, where she has over sixty thousand followers. Her red rabbits and other creatures travel the world. The majority of her clients are buying paintings for the first time—they'd never been interested in art before, but found themselves hypnotized by her strange images. "This American girl bought a rabbit for one of her friends, but while she was waiting to give it to him, she realized that she needed a red rabbit of her own," Marina said. "I've gotten a huge amount of positive feedback. I don't even understand why people love them so much."

I read about fifty books in English over the past year, and not a single one in Russian.
divulge — разглашать
malevolent — злой, злорадный
febrile — лихорадочный
abrasive — колкий, резкий
thaw — оттепель
nebula — туманность
parsimony — жадность, скупость
assent — согласие, одобрение
elate — поднимать настроение, ободрять
billow
abide
expel — исключать, изгонять
plod — звук шагов
infer — заключать, делать вывод
retain — сохранять
concede — уступать
desolate
maverick — независимый человек
flair — нюх, чутье
elate — поднимать настроение
yield
sly
vex

For many years, Marina was politically active, painting posters and attending mass protests. Sometimes, she's sad that she has left all that behind: activism and barricades are important, she thinks, while surrealist art has no concrete social purpose.

"I don't have any problems with this regime," Marina said. "But I worry that others do. When I see the Rosgvardia at protests, I feel like enemy forces are occupying my city. It's very scary and terrible. I'm also afraid of the police. Policemen are supposed to help us, but actually, in Russia, they're here to make our lives worse."

Listening to Marina, I thought about how her art wasn't all that surrealistic. I feel like Marina and I are drawing the same dark forest: the lack of rights, the humiliation, the fear that surrounds us. Like little invisible animals, we hide in the forest in our little holes, under the tree roots. But we are red.

The second artist I visited was Sergey Skutaru, who lives in Zelenograd, a small town outside Moscow. I had been interested in his paintings for a long time. I'd seen them online but never in person and we didn't know each other. Here's what I knew about him: he was self-taught, he was born in Moldova in 1979, he'd come to Russia twenty years earlier as a migrant worker, he'd been married and was now widowed.

It turned out that Sergey lives in a one-room apartment with two teenage daughters. "This is my sanctuary," he said, pointing to the small kitchen. "It's where I sleep, cook, and draw." Instead of a kitchen table, the room had a narrow bed. There was no room for an easel, for sketchbooks, or for stretcher bars. Sergey's paintings were tacked to the wall.

I asked Skutaru to show me his work. He led me into the living room, where he began taking rolled-up canvases down from the shelves. I saw self-portraits, portraits of his daughters, images of an unsettled living situation, views of the completely unremarkable Zelenograd. These simple subjects were represented with so much energy that the paintings looked like they were of bombs going off. The people looked like the characters from *Twin Peaks* who only pretend to be people. The objects in his still lives came to life: a folding cot with a flowery bedspread turned into a flowerbed overgrown with wild plants; the dirty dishes were somehow moving around in the sink; a red and blue backpack looked ready to pounce like a venomous reptile.

—The gaze transforms objects. I want to see something beyond the insignificance of my subjects.

I love the Kind of Russian culture where everything is calm on the outside, but the soul is roiling within.

We drank wine in the kitchen. Skutaru sat on his bed, and I took the chair. The windowsill was the table. The artist told me that he feels depressed that Russia keeps getting more isolated from the rest of the world. He'd recently learned that yet another one of our mutual friends had been declared a foreign agent—things like that scared him. "We need to live our own lives, ignoring the state," I said. "That's what everyone did in the final years of the Soviet Union. The Soviet Union fell apart in a single instant."

It was snowing outside, but you could still see a few things: a ravine, the occasional passerby, the brown high-rises. "I look at this building," said Sergey. "A hulk of concrete. Red and brown. You can feel that color spattering at you—you can feel it on your skin. That's live realism."

I could tell that this lonely artist actually liked the dark energy of these areas. He liked the drama. What do I like? I knew for sure that I no longer wanted to be the Last Soviet Artist. I'll finish this book and that will be that.

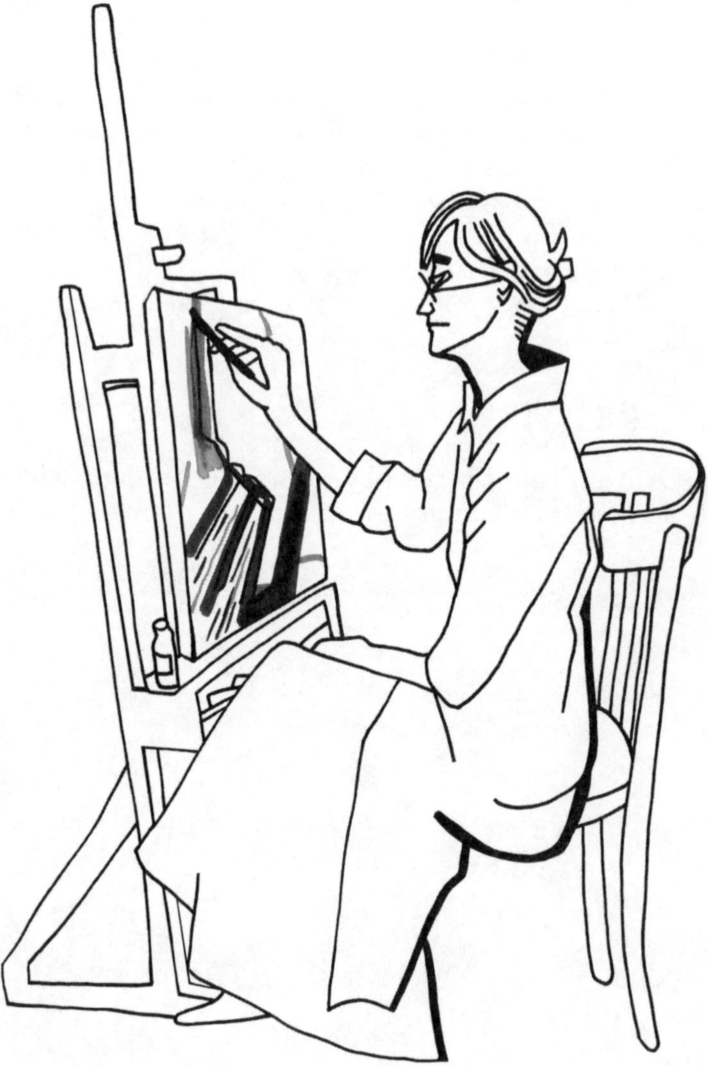

My third visit was to my close friend Nadia Plungian, who lives in Veshnyaki. To many people, Veshnyaki is a completely anonymous neighborhood in the backstreets of Moscow, but Nadia considers it magical—full of poetry. "Buildings like this remind me of constructivism. I feel like I'm living in one of Malevich's suprematist paintings," Nadia said of her totally regular high-rise, built in the 1970s.

Those who know of Plungian know her as one of the most famous art historians and curators in Russia. Only her closest friends know that Nadia is also a serious painter. She used to make figurative, symbolic paintings with coded scenes from her life, but during the pandemic, Nadia suddenly turned to abstraction, most reminiscent of music seen from within. Here she is sitting at her easel, making mysterious marks on her canvas.

Sometimes I think that Nadia is more of a true artist than I am. My father, a provincial artist with huge, unrealized ambitions, forced me to draw. Since I was little, I was accustomed to seeing visual art as the craft that I would use to support myself. In reality, as a child, I preferred writing poems and stories. But being an artist seemed more promising than something as vague as a writer.

Nadia's parents, successful Moscow professors, were categorically opposed to her going to art school and painting. Very slowly, step by step, Nadia overcame her irrational fears from childhood, fears that gotten in the way of her becoming immersed in art. But now, this space is not clouded by worries over her career, anxiety over selling work or competing with other artists.

—True art is the key to the future.

From 2012 until 2014, Nadia and I co-curated the Feminist Pencil, a project that was radical in Russia at the time. In our feminist art shows, Nadia showed her work—queer feminist and antiwar posters and banners—under a pseudonym. Eventually, she started to get deeper into a kind of art that attempts to see into the future, rather than describing already existing facts. I stayed in the role of the socially engaged artist for a long time, focusing on hot-button issues.

During the pandemic, I was mad at Nadia for not going to opposition protests anymore, but now, I don't want to go to them, either. It's not an artist's job to run from the police clutching her sketchbook—her job is to draw the outlines of the future she wants to see, helping to manifest it. We are much more needed in our studios than we are in the fray.

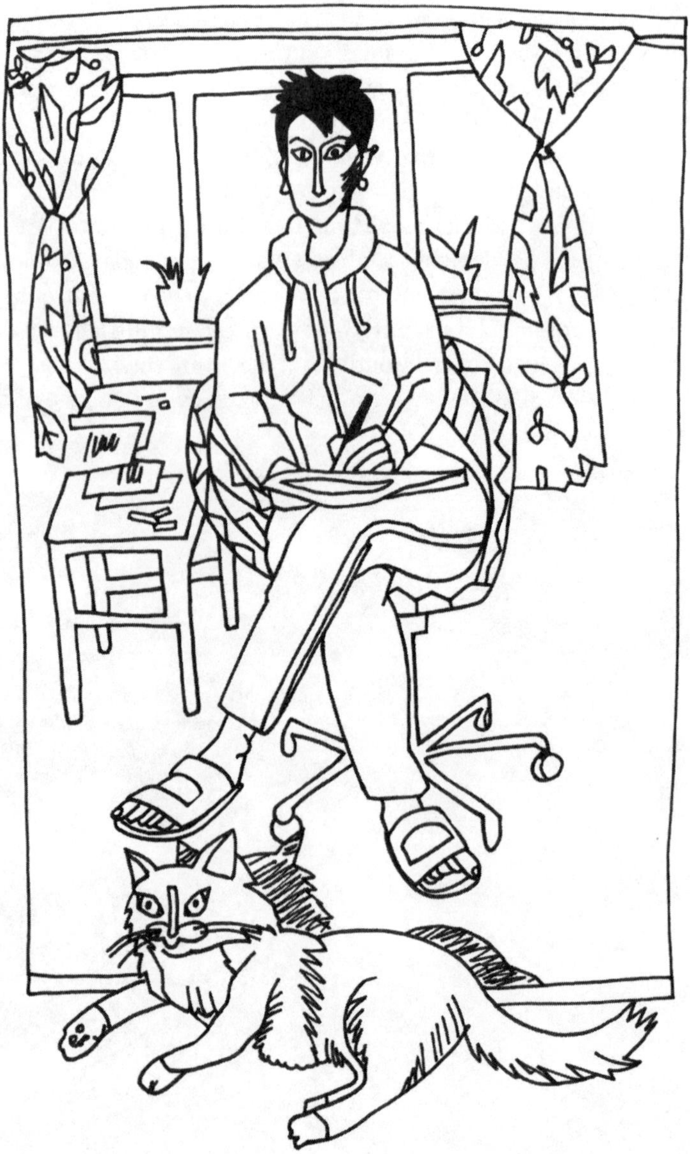

The last artist I want to talk about in this chapter is me. I was born in the Soviet Union, and despite the fact that it fell apart when I was a teenager, the experience of living in a totalitarian state isolated from the rest of the world is something that's stayed with me. More than anything in the world, I never want to live like that again.

In the spring of 2020, as the pandemic broke out, I returned to Russia after working on a project in the West. That first year, when the borders were all closed, wasn't that psychologically challenging. In the second year, the majority of countries remained closed to Russians, primarily because the Russian vaccine hadn't been approved by the WHO and foreign vaccines were forbidden in Russia. Your worst fears have a way of coming true: there I was, a hostage of other people's political disagreements.

I spent these two pandemic years in my small apartment; one of my two rooms is my studio. I thought about art, changed my artistic language, edited and finished *The Last Soviet Artist.* It was difficult editing the first part. It felt like the chapters had been composed by some stranger who'd put together the "right" elements like a puzzle: activists and feminists, the history of social inequality, and examples of civic initiatives. In reality, my useful art, with its socially conscious, pro-West messaging, was not so different from the propaganda paintings my father, a book designer, had been forced to make in Soviet times: Lenin, workers, Young Pioneers, the bright communist future, enemy capitalists. My father had served a regime he despised, while I was attempting to fight the present regime, critiquing it based on Western values. That's how my life was passing.

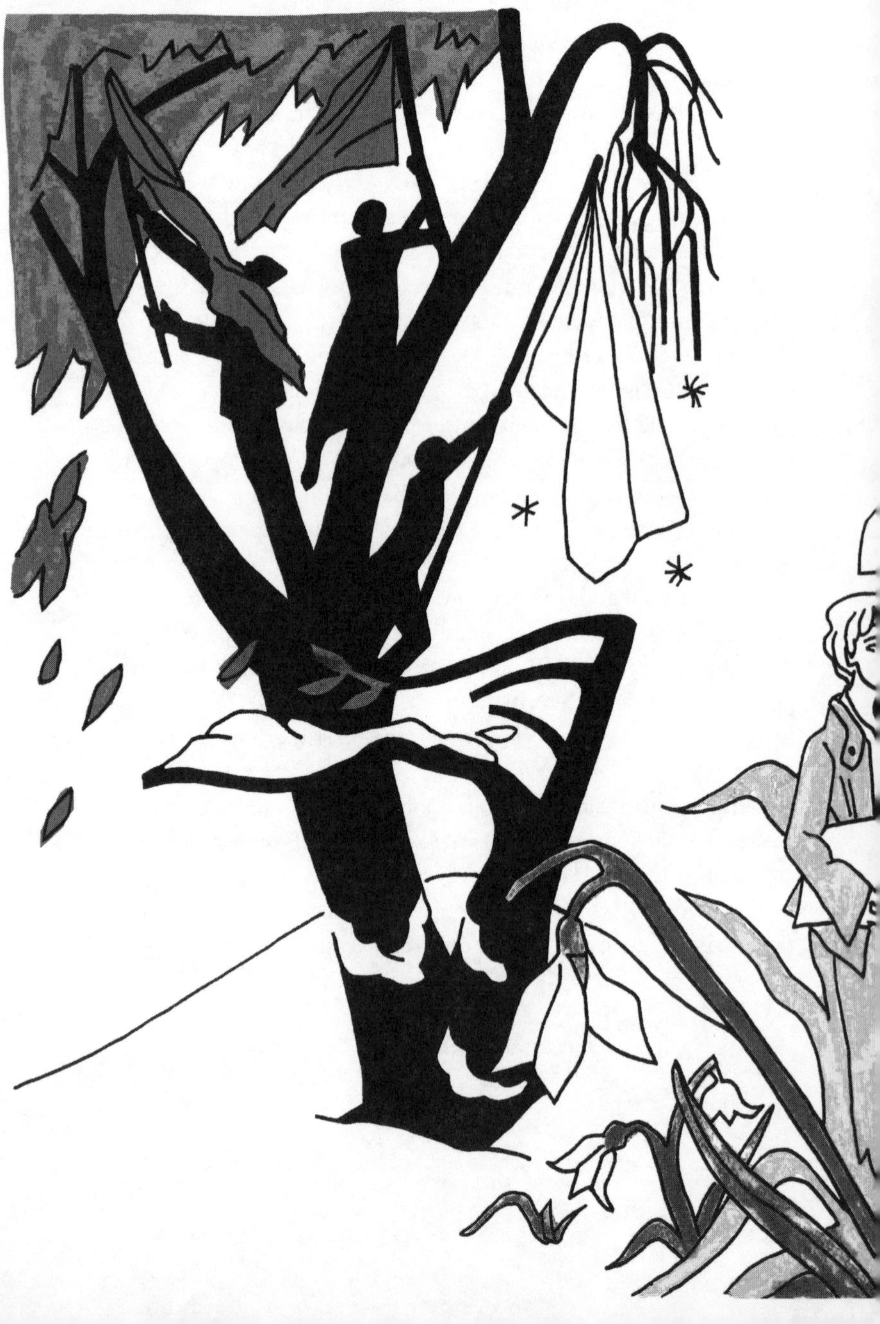

The author writing this book doesn't fight or criticize. I see a changing of the epochs happening in front of me, and I am just observing these phenomena, as natural as the change of the seasons. It doesn't matter what is or isn't happening around me—what is important is my internal state, how deeply I can get into the heart of things. I'm glad to be parting ways with the tedious Last Soviet Artist for whom political developments were more important that the first flowers coming up in the courtyard. Up ahead lie the fantastical and emotional worlds of Victoria Lomasko, unfurling independently of anyone else in the world.

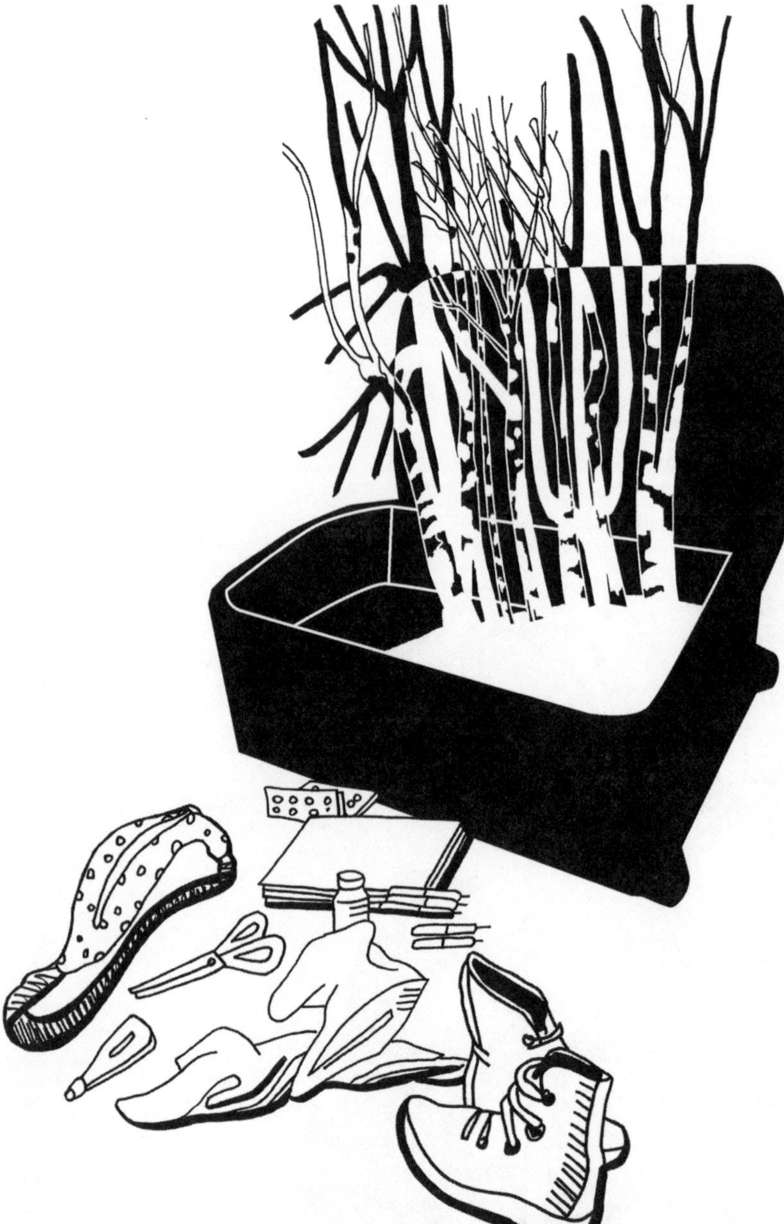

EXILE

MOSCOW UNDER SNOW

MOSCOW UNDER SNOW
by Victoria Lomasko
In February of 2022 I started to draw this comic about a snow-covered Moscow.
SALE!
On Izmaylovsky Island, near my house, children were rolling down its hills on whatever they could find and laughing.
Then one day I woke up in my city and heard the news: Putin had started a "special military operation" in Ukraine.

My neighbor and I think the same way, but if we publicly call this war a war, we could get 15 years in prison.
It's not my war. This is Putin's war.
After five hours of waiting in line at my bank, I found out I can only withdraw the savings I had in Euros in Rubles.
Because of the sanctions, the Rubles had turned into garbage.
It is 3am. My last meeting with my friends. We all heard the news that Russia is bombing Kharkiv and can't sleep.
According to the new laws, I am a foreign agent who worked for enemy states. This is my last sketch at my home. The unknown lies ahead.
MOIST

COLLECTIVE SHAME
(WITH JOE SACCO)

COLLECTIVE SHAME
WRITTEN BY VICTORIA LOMASKO, ART BY JOE SACCO 2022
MY NAME IS JOE, AND HERE I'M GOING TO BE VICTORIA LOMASKO'S PEN.
VICTORIA IS A RUSSIAN ARTIST, WHO IN HER HASTE, HAD TO LEAVE ALL HER ART SUPPLIES BEHIND IN MOSCOW. THE WORDS HERE ARE HERS.
VLADIMIR PUTIN'S INVASION OF UKRAINE IS, ABOVE ALL, A CATASTROPHE FOR THE UKRAINIAN PEOPLE, BUT IT HAS ALSO TRANSFORMED THE LIVES OF MANY RUSSIANS.
There was anxiety and despair at the airport as people left for any destination possible.
Most people were fleeing not from sanctions but from dictatorship.
Once I felt like I was a worldly artist. Now I'm a refugee — with one suitcase and a cat named Dwarf.
It was only when I got to Western Europe that I realized the scale of the sanctions on all Russians.
I CAN'T USE MY RUSSIAN SAVINGS AND I CAN'T OPEN AN ACCOUNT IN BELGIUM, EITHER.
RUSSIAN PASSPORT
ARTISTS AROUND THE WORLD HAD NEARLY ALWAYS BEEN SUPPORTIVE, BUT INSTITUTIONS ARE NOW RELUCTANT TO ENGAGE WITH ANYONE RUSSIAN.

FOR THE PAST TEN YEARS, I HAVE BEEN DRAWING PICTURES OF PEOPLE AT PROTESTS.
РОССИЯ БЕЗ ПУТИНА
Most young Russians consider themselves part of Europe and want to live free from violence.
МОЯ РОССИЯ СИДИТ В ТЮРЬМЕ
ХВАТИТ ЗАЩИЩАТЬ ПРЕСТУПНУЮ ВЛАСТЬ
But the majority of Russian society absorbs and repeats state propaganda.
EVERYTHING IS CENSORED. YOU CAN GO TO JAIL FOR YEARS IF YOU POST SOMETHING CRITICAL ON SOCIAL MEDIA.
Яндекс Такси
On my last day in Moscow, I was in a cab. On the radio, there was a warning.
ОМОН
DUE TO THE COVID-19 PANDEMIC, IT IS ILLEGAL TO ENCOURAGE PARTICIPATION IN UNAUTHORIZED PUBLIC EVENTS AND TO PARTICIPATE IN SUCH DEMONSTRATIONS.

WHILE I WAS STILL IN RUSSIA, I GOT MESSAGES ON INSTAGRAM FROM A UKRAINIAN ARTIST WHO'S BEEN LIVING IN BERLIN.
I hope you plan to protest.
And that 15 days in jail doesn't scare you.
But, for the first time, I was afraid to go and be branded a "foreign agent" working for "enemy" Western countries...
НЕТ ВОЙНЕ С УКРАИНОЙ
ПУТИ
ГРОБЫ
... WHILE THOSE COUNTRIES HAVE NEARLY CLOSED THEIR MINDS TO ANYONE WHO HAPPENS TO BE RUSSIAN.
A friend who goes to rallies says that his legs shake with fear. Maybe he'll get fifteen days, maybe years.
The new laws are vague. But for sure he'll be humiliated, likely beaten and detained.
Those who oppose the war might find their door marked by the letter "Z."
"Z": THE UBIQUITOUS NEW SYMBOL INDICATING SUPPORT FOR THE INVASION
The Western public hopes for mass protests.
ПРОСТИ НАС УКРАИНА
УКРАИНА ТЫ ПРАВ
НЕТ ВОЙНЕ
But they see that only a small minority dares take to the streets.

Every day, the Russian Army kills Ukrainian soldiers and civilians.

Whole cities have been reduced to rubble.

IN THE FACE OF SUCH DEATH AND DESTRUCTION, HOW CAN ANYONE COMPLAIN ABOUT BEING BOYCOTTED OR SANCTIONED?

MOST OF US WHO ARE AGAINST THE WAR DO NOT.

AS A HOLDER OF A RUSSIAN PASSPORT, I'M READY TO ACCEPT THOSE PENALTIES.

BUT, AS AN ARTIST, I AM STRUGGLING TO FIND MY VOICE.

For many years now, I've been drawing stories of ordinary Russians and describing the choices they've made in their lives.

AFTER VICTORIA LOMASKO

BUT WHAT CHOICES ARE THERE...

FOR SOMEONE CAUGHT BETWEEN PUTIN, SHAME AT THE WAR, AND WHAT FEELS LIKE WESTERN REJECTION OF ALL RUSSIANS?

FIVE STEPS

1. ISOLATION

I was born in a closed, totalitarian country. One would think that as long as a child didn't know any other reality, they could be happy. Here I am flipping through the pages of a children's magazine for early readers: I study the pretty pictures and read the propaganda—stories about the USSR and its pioneers and heroes. Here I am at school: I've forgotten my red tie and am sent home to retrieve it. Here I am in the assembly hall after school, where the whole class has been forced to march and sing patriotic songs: there's a Soviet holiday coming up and preparations are underway. I don't want to march. I say that I have a headache, that I'm about to faint. I beg to be sent home.

My dad hates communism and makes a living drawing communist propaganda. My parents attend meetings after work, cheer at demonstrations, and give up the occasional Saturday to volunteer for the cause. I remember hundreds of details of everyday life in the Soviet Union, but how to convey what seems most important?

I'm on a high-speed train traveling from Brussels to Frankfurt. Two Europeans my age sit across from me. They smile when my gaze rests on them. Their faces are relaxed, their bodies loose and free. They have the look of people who have never known humiliation.

Life in a closed, totalitarian country means that you'll inevitably come up against humiliation, which is itself a form of control and punishment. You can be talented, cheerful, brave—but if you contravene the system it will destroy you. You think about the fact that years before you were born, a group of politicians closed off the rest of the world to you: you can fantasize, speculate, assemble a picture in your mind based on movies and photos and stories told by strangers, but you'll never encounter the world you've been cut off from. You'll never taste it for yourself. The USSR collapsed in 1991, but I never lost the fear that I would again end up in a closed country where my life would be controlled by other people.

After my book was published in the US in 2017, I became a well-known writer. My work wasn't published or shown in Russia because of censorship, so I started to exhibit and lecture in Europe, the US, and the UK. Even before the war in Ukraine and the subsequent sanctions regime imposed on Russian citizens it was hard to get a visa with a Russian passport. At the same time, every new bit of success—the publication of the book, a big gallery show—made returning home more dangerous. By 2019 it was becoming very difficult to balance life in Russia with my work abroad.

All my visas lapsed after the pandemic began in 2020, and it was impossible for me to acquire any new ones because I didn't have access to foreign vaccines. So I spent two years in Russia without ever leaving. I roamed around my neighborhood in search of subjects for new work. I lived in Moscow, in a Khrushchyovka—a type of five-story building constructed in the 1960s across the country. The Khrushchyovkas in my neighborhood are faced with gray brick, and the impression one gets walking around is of moving through an endless gray light. Not far from my house is the enormous Izmailovo Hotel, opened in 1980. The concert hall enfolded by the complex is encircled by a bronze frieze that depicts similar-looking muscular athletes running, swimming, and jumping with parachutes. The space between them is taken up by waves, birds, and five-pointed stars. A bit farther down is the Izmailovo flea market, whose towers and turrets imitate the architecture of the Russian past and the baroque style of the 17th century. I looked out at this landscape and had the sense that time was bending backward—that the roofs of the Khrushchyovkas were being overgrown with moss and little towers and churches were pushing through.

I was frightened by the number of posters I saw reminding everyone that we had been the victors in World War II. On the subway I occasionally ended up on the so-called Victory Train, which was decorated with photos of Soviet soldiers holding automatic rifles and anti-fascist posters. At first I tried to avoid the warning signs, but then I decided to describe and depict them. A number of times I went out of my way to visit the Patriot Park museum complex, where tanks are lined up in endless rows and the huge expanse is dotted with militaristic statues. At the park's entrance is the Main Cathedral of the Russian Armed Forces, which resembles a horror movie castle. It was there that I understood that the Putin regime would pull us inevitably into a new war. It was there that I found the subjects for my new work: the gloomy forest, whose branches transform into automatic weapons and Soviet monuments that come alive to take revenge.

2. ESCAPE

On February 24 I woke up at home in Moscow and read the news that Putin had begun the war in Ukraine. From that moment on, all my thoughts were focused on only one thing: how to leave the country.

That same day, the dictatorship in Russia clarified itself. The center of Moscow was occupied by prisoner transport vehicles and the black cars of the National Guard raced through the streets with their sirens blaring. I heard announcements on the radio that any gatherings of people were banned "due to the tense Covid-19 situation."

There were constant news stories about arrests, and even on public transportation, in cafés, and in line you could hear fragments of conversations about people being searched and apprehended just for daring to say something against the war.

I overheard one conversation while waiting in line at the bank, where I spent a few hours hoping to withdraw euros from my account. A young woman was telling her elderly mother about women with children arrested at antiwar protests—she was also planning to attend the demonstration.

"Spring is here," her mother said, trying to change the subject.

"War is here," the daughter responded.

"We're lucky that we managed to live for at least a little while without war," the mother said.

I understood that if I stayed in Russia the police would soon break into my apartment. They would rifle through my drawings, read my writing, and destroy my archive. There is no justice in Russia: I could be imprisoned for three years, or maybe a decade. Putin could announce martial law at any time. He could close the borders. I began to have panic attacks. I had to change my shirt and my socks three times per day. My body was covered in a cold sweat. It would have been easier for me to run in the middle of a crowd, to throw stones and try to burn down everything in my way than to feel . . . how did I feel, exactly? The whole time I kept thinking of the footage from Kabul International Airport in 2021: the last airplane takes off and a crowd of people hoping to escape into the free and open world is left behind on the runway.

I managed to leave Russia on a short-term tourist visa. As I write this I'm on my seventh month in the European Union. The panic attacks haven't gone away. The most recent one occurred when I read an article in the *Washington Post* titled "Zelensky calls on West to ban all Russian travelers." "Whichever kind of Russian . . . make them go to Russia," Zelensky said. When I read that I started feeling dizzy and wanted to throw up. It wasn't enough that Putin had broken my life—now the so-called collective West would uphold the punishment? I decided that if I was ever able to come back to Russia, I would try to work with the younger generation—to teach them how to defend their freedom, and also never to trust the West.

When I finally calmed down a little I thought about what this collective "West" Russians have heard so much about actually represents. How is this community different from the one referred to as "Russians"? Some politicians demand that people be punished on the basis of their passports, some institutions boycott them based on backgrounds they can't do anything about, some media organizations launch smear campaigns, and some countries close their borders and cancel visas. All this has happened, and at the same time the French Embassy in Moscow was able to give me a visa in a single day, a few hours before my flight, and later helped me transport my entire archive to Europe. The Vrije Universiteit Brussel and the Université libre de Bruxelles helped me exhibit a new antiwar mural in the center of Brussels. The Akademie Schloss Solitude in Germany gave me a fellowship. My Western publishers, producers, and gallerists supported me over the past few months and became real friends, rather than merely colleagues. So it is up to me whether I want to focus on the people who seek to judge and punish me, or those who want to support and help.

Here's what I'd say to President Zelensky: There's room for an artist or a writer everywhere. This entire world is mine by birthright.

3. EXILE

Why didn't I bring my favorite calligraphy pens with me? Why didn't I bring my favorite drawing pens? That tiny pen box wouldn't have taken much room in my suitcase. I'm standing in the middle of Schleiper, a huge art supply store in Brussels. It's my second day in Belgium and I've come to buy drawing materials.

When tragedy strikes, rational thought is abandoned. I don't think about the elderly parents I've left behind; about the friends in danger in Russia; about my Moscow apartment, which I'd transformed over the years into a cozy workshop. I think about my pen box.

I don't remember when I first held a calligraphy pen and began to draw in ink. I must have been 8 years old. It was my father who gave me the pen box. Before the Soviet Union fell he worked as a graphic designer in the Metallist plant in Serpukhov. He used these calligraphy pens to sketch posters that were produced for communist holidays. When the Soviet Union broke apart and all the artists were fired, he brought home a few boxes he'd been given at the plant. They were supposed to last him—and me—the rest of our lives. And here I am in this enormous store, and I can't find the right kind of pens. Everything I try produces totally different lines.

I began adding text to my graphic reportage in 2007, and at the time I couldn't imagine how far that would take me. At first I simply drew people in public places, listening in on their conversations and transcribing them as they happened. Eventually I began to understand that there are hundreds and hundreds of important stories happening all at once—happening right now—and if I didn't try to capture them, no one would.

In 2009 I went to draw the trial of the curators of an art exhibition called *Forbidden Art*, which displayed work that had been banned and censored at other exhibitions. The case had been cooked up by Russian Orthodox activists. In the course of drawing the trial I received the first threats I'd ever gotten—the activists promised to come to my home and lie in wait for me, to "draw all over me" so hard that I wouldn't be able to draw my own work. There were many days in the courtroom when there was no one on the defense side other than me. Returning home with new drawings in my backpack, I felt afraid.

Over the next decade and beyond, I drew the residents of Russia's provinces, the pupils of its juvenile prisons, the teachers and students of its rural schools, its sex workers, its lesbian couples, its activists, its citizens who participated in opposition protests and protest camps.

I also drew numerous political trials, each of which ended with the punishment of the opponents of Putin's regime. I tried to give these opponents a voice, to make them visible. Now I carry all these people and their stories in my heart. And while the Western media expects Russian dissidents to publicly condemn the entire Russian people, I have no plans to betray them.

A few days ago the mobilization began in Russia. The first order of business is to catch men who live in the provinces, especially in regions with sizable minority ethnic populations. Women, old men, and children are thus left all alone. People who could barely get by as it is now don't know what to do. And somewhere far away, in a world that's unfathomable and inaccessible to these people, European politicians discuss how to punish them so comprehensively that they finally depose the Putin regime. To oppose such a dictatorship, a person has to be ready for death. This is the kind of decision that every person has to make for themselves.

4. SHAME

The depths of night. I'm sitting at a desk that's not my own and making sketches of antiwar murals. Suddenly my friend A. starts to scream. She's seven months pregnant. We're in a little mansard apartment that belongs to the friends of our producer—we've been settled here. We escaped from Moscow together: Moscow–Bishkek–Istanbul–Paris–Brussels.

A. really didn't want to leave. She loves Russia, Moscow, and the father of her child. But he has participated in every single antiwar and anti-government action and has been arrested a number of times. The next time it happens he'll face criminal charges. A. spent days waiting for the doorbell to ring, or for the FSB to simply break down her door. After that she went in for a checkup and was told by her doctor that her baby's heartbeat was inaudible. A. was sure she was about to lose consciousness. In the end the doctor determined that her child was still alive. After that, A. decided to escape with me. She didn't have any money. Our debit cards no longer worked on the other side of the border because of the sanctions, and A. wasn't able to withdraw any euros from her online bank in Russia because the ATMs were out of money. Her insurance didn't cover her in Europe, so she wouldn't be able to see a doctor easily.

And now she's screaming as if someone were murdering her, and I—the person who persuaded her to run—am frantically searching the internet, trying to figure out what can help pregnant people when their legs cramp. I apply some wet rags and look for the phone number of the local ambulance service. We don't end up calling, though. What if the service isn't free? We have nothing with which to pay them.

Every morning in Brussels, A. would head off to a studio on the other side of town, where she was editing her new documentary. I spent entire days sitting in the mansard room drawing sketches for a mural and comics and caricatures about the war in Ukraine and the dictatorship in Russia. A. would return in the evening and I'd make pasta with ground beef. A. always knew the latest news of the war, and of course I did, too. As soon as she entered the room we would launch into frantic discussions of what was happening that day in Russia and Ukraine. It seemed that the ruins of bombed houses and the bodies of the dead were present in our midst, invisible but inescapable.

What did we feel? Anguish. Grief. Shame that the criminal Putin regime was committing all these new crimes in the name of Russian citizens. Did we feel collective guilt? I didn't. For over a decade I'd done as much as a political artist could. A. didn't feel guilty, either. She was born in the provinces and had worked hard to get to Moscow. She financed her own social and political filmmaking, worked with migrants from Central Asia, and participated in every possible protest action. Even so, as we sat at someone else's table eating our pasta, it seemed to us that we were in the presence of shadows—the shadows of people fleeing the bombing in Ukraine.

When, two months later, it was time for A. to give birth, she set off for a local hospital that served the homeless, migrants, and other vulnerable groups, hoping to get free medical care there. After spending the entire day in line, she couldn't make any headway. A few days later her tourist visa ran out and she became illegal. In the end she did end up giving birth at that hospital—and subsequently received an enormous bill. At the time of this writing she's planning to return to Moscow, where her home was the target of a police raid: they were looking for her partner.

5. HUMANITY

When I hear the calls to "cancel" Russian culture, I think: Go ahead and kill me, too. I have no other path, no other identity besides being an artist. I can't change my blood, and you'll never grant me any citizenship. I've become increasingly certain that I've spent my entire life drawing a single work of art—one that takes as its subject freedom of choice and the uniqueness of every individual. If I'd been born in the US, or China, or Iran, or anywhere else, I'd be doing the same thing. All that would change would be the names of people and the backdrops.

What is a nationality? If an activist who comes out against the war and the police officer with a Z on his back who beats him up are the same entity, then that entity must also include in its ranks all the Western politicians and businesspeople who have collaborated with the Putin regime for decades. It includes the Western intelligentsia now practicing its selective so-called humanism.

"Everything is so fucked up right now," a German friend wrote to me. "All kinds of values we relied on no longer seem to apply." This friend has always focused on political art and fighting censorship—throughout her career she has cooperated with artists in the line of fire. These days when I read the Russian press and the Western press, I sense that they're united in one key respect: everyone seems to think that in a time of war, real humanism is too great a luxury.

When we're involved in larger historical processes, every person's choices fall somewhere on a spectrum that includes crime, indifference, and heroism. It is obvious that a person who calls for murder and destruction in Ukraine and a person who helps refugees in Russia at great personal risk represent two absolutely different universes. Behind these choices is someone's entire life: the millions of little choices made up to that moment.

Geopolitical games that operate on the basis of clear distinctions between good nationalities and bad ones cannot lead anywhere healthy. But the idea of a single humanity composed of unique individuals is a pledge toward collective progress. I worry that there are many difficult challenges ahead, and only once we pass through them will we recognize that we are one. Still, I'm not envious of those whose position is more stable than mine. The changes we face are so enormous that there will be only one way to approach the future: with empty hands.